THE COMPLETE ESL FOR BEGINNERS:

Lessons Guide with Activities Volumes One through Three

A Comprehensive Guide for Teaching Beginning English to Speakers of Other Languages

Stephanie Lerner, MS
Texas-Certified Bilingual Educator

This book is dedicated to Silvestre and our talented English student-teachers of teams *Never Go Back*, *Go On*, and *Spiritual Volunteers*. May your future English students inspire you as you all have inspired me.

Future English Students in Chimoio, Mozambique

Like and follow Bilingual Learner on our pages below to see our weekly posts/photos on developments in the ESL world and to receive our newest free/low-cost products!
www.instagram.com/bilinguallearner/
www.bilinguallearner.com
www.facebook.com/bilinguallearn
www.twitter.com/bilinguallearn

Published by Bilingual Learner, LLC.
Logo design by Michell Schalik.

Printed in the United States of America.
First Printing 2013

For information on this publication or others by this author, visit **www.bilinguallearner.com** or e-mail the author at **bilinguallearner@hotmail.com**.
Special discounts are available on quantity orders.

Table of Contents

Recommendations for Teaching *ESL for Beginners*

Writing this lessons guide has been a real labor of love, built on all my past beginning ESL/EFL (English as a Second Language or Foreign Language) teaching adventures. Over the last 15 years, I have spent time teaching English to people from all different walks of life: young children in a Bolivian orphanage, private school students in an American-International school, adults at a teachers' college in Africa, and children at various Mozambican public schools. These adventures have led me to my current work with adolescent "newcomers" in the Texas public school system where I teach afterschool beginner ESL classes. For all of these groups, I used many of the same activities—obviously tweaked a bit to fit the different cultures and age groups. So, *The Complete ESL for Beginners Lessons Guide* that you have in your hands is many years in the making, involving many trips down memory lane to revisit my days of teaching ESL/EFL in order to gather up all the activities that comprise these 60 different lesson plans. And, as you might be able to tell from the book dedication, my memories have settled the most on my time in Africa…to my days of working with my *Never Go Back* group in the mountains of the Mozambican town of Chimoio in 2003. This was the name my adult Mozambican students adopted for themselves after their beginning English class to show the world that they were "never going back" to being non-English speakers. Their enthusiasm and pride in achieving a basic foundation in speaking the English language was a joy to see. Even now, 10 years later, it still gives me such a warm feeling to think back on their dedication to learning English that had them bounding into my class at the start of the next semester to pick up where they had left off with their language learning. I hope your students will do the same!

Here are the practices that work best with all my different groups of students:

- Included in this guide are 60 beginner-level lessons. They can be taught over any time span, but for the fastest English acquisition, I recommend meeting with students Monday–Friday for about 1–3 hours to teach this guide at the pace of one lesson per day. Be sure to give a 10-minute break per hour. You can then end your English class for the day or extend it by using one of the field trip ideas from Appendix M. If you follow this schedule, the lessons guide should take about 3 months to complete. If you would like to continue to use this series to teach your ESL students, you can find *ESL in the Middle, Volume One* at the website **www.bilinguallearner.com**.
- The acronyms ESL and EFL have slightly different connotations; mainly that ESL is primarily used for teaching English in a country where the national language is English and EFL is used for teaching English in a country that does not have English as its national language. However, for the sake of simplicity, this guide will use the term ESL for both acronyms.
- As noted above, each lesson can be lengthened or shortened because many of the activities naturally allow for this. For example, you can sing all the songs or play multiple games in one lesson to lengthen the lesson time to 3 hours. Conversely, you can split a "Create Your Own Dialogue" activity over two days, with the students creating/practicing their dialogues the first day and presenting them the second day in order to shorten the lesson.
- These lessons are appropriate for ages eight to adult; however, here are some tips on using this guide with very young or with adult students:

-You might simplify some of the written activities so very young students can repeat/copy your example, rather than read on their own.

-You might skip some of the lengthy rules in the more advanced structures of this guide for very young students. Instead, spend this extra time as follows:

- Practice the structure by pronouncing additional sentences/question examples with the class.
- Have students do more of the corresponding games/activities for that structure's content.

-If you are concerned that some of the songs, games, and activities may be too juvenile for your adult students, here are some tips:

- Keep in mind that this a guide for beginner-level students trying to master English speaking and listening, rather than for business or medical students studying advanced, professional English.
- Also keep in mind that the teacher always sets the tone for the class; therefore, if you are enthusiastic and comfortable with the activities, your students will be too. Likewise, if you feel awkward, juvenile, and unconfident about singing and playing games with your students, your class will mirror these feelings.

- For ESL classes in a general education school setting where you don't have a formal district-wide process for identifying English language learners, set up your ESL resource group of students by asking for teacher referrals of the students who are struggling the most with speaking/understanding English in their classrooms. Once you have a list of students to work with, send home the parent notification letter (Appendix A) and assess each student (Appendix B) for grouping and data purposes.
- Begin your class with an assessment (Appendix B) so you have a baseline of each student's English language skills; if you give the same assessment at the end of this curriculum, you can determine how much progress has been made and where he/she needs further support. There are also informal assessments built into every lesson through games, the Circle Speaking Activity, the structures independent practice, etc.
- I usually divide students into groups by the English Speaking Levels (beginning, intermediate, advanced) listed in Appendix B. Occasionally, I run two different groups for the BES students (beginners) if there are students who have never spoken/heard English AND students who have a basic English foundation.
- It is important to use the songs, games, Circle Time activities, video clips, chapter books, etc. to spiral the teaching/learning. This means integrating daily reviews of previously taught concepts into your lessons. You will find a lot of repetition across lessons and this is purposeful—learning requires repetition and review. And language learning, in particular, requires a lot of it! Incidentally, Circle Time is perfectly appropriate for the little ones all the way up to adults. I have small children sit on the floor in a circle around me, while older children and adults sit around me in chairs.
- I've found that the best way to communicate with students is to speak clearly and slowly, repeat everything twice, and throw in just the tiniest bit of native language only when absolutely necessary.

- When having students read aloud, I like to work in a round-robin fashion—meaning that students read a portion aloud as we come to them, moving clockwise around the circle. I explain at the beginning of every lesson that anyone who doesn't want to read aloud can just say "pass."
- When working on speaking chorally with students, here are the steps I follow:
  1. I pronounce the letter/sound/sentence while they listen only.
  2. I pronounce it again and have the students repeat what I've said.
  3. We pronounce it together.
  4. They pronounce it as a group without me.
- Each day I start off the lesson referring to chart paper or the chalk/whiteboard where I've written the day of the week, the date with month/day/year, and a list of our day's activities. Here's how I introduce this:
  1. I read what is written, and they listen to the pronunciation.
  2. We read it together.
  3. A student translates it so everyone understands the day's activities.
- Throughout this guide, there are many opportunities to teach students new vocabulary. Please refer to Appendix R if you need creative ideas on how to quickly introduce new vocabulary to students.
- Total physical response (TPR) is a great teaching technique that helps facilitate language acquisition. In TPR, the student uses his/her body to act out a concept being taught. For example, while the teacher reads aloud a story about wind, the students might sway back and forth when the wind blows in the story.
- I make sure my students have lots of opportunities to earn prizes during lessons and games. The chance to win a prize is very motivating at any age, so I give prizes to the big kids and adults too. In all my years working with kids and adults alike, I've never had anyone turn down a prize.
- This lessons guide combines excellently with the culture group sessions guides, *ESL for Beginners – Culture Explorers* or *ESL Survival Skills – Exploring U.S. Culture*. With these cultural guides, you can lead your students on an exploration of the traditions and lifestyle of the English-speaking or American cultures. You can find this guide and other products at **www.bilinguallearner.com**.

TESOL Standards-Based Language Functions and Topics

The organization called Teaching English to Speakers of Other Languages (TESOL) sets the national and international framework for an exceptional English as a Second Language educational program. As a part of this framework, TESOL has created their English Language Proficiency Standards (ELPS) to guide the ESL student to mastery of the English language. Standard 1 relates to using English to communicate socially, interculturally, and for instructional purposes. Because the focus of *ESL for Beginners, Volume One* is to strengthen English speaking and listening skills, our lesson objectives are based on the following TESOL Standard 1 Language Functions and Topics.

STANDARD 1: English language learners communicate for SOCIAL, INTERCULTURAL, and INSTRUCTIONAL PURPOSES within the school setting.

Goal 1: To use English to communicate in social settings

Language Functions and Topics

Describe feelings and emotions
Indicate interests, opinions, or preferences
Give and ask for permission
Offer and respond to greetings, compliments, invitations, introductions, and farewells
Clarify and restate information
Use the primary language to ask for clarification
Use context to construct meaning
Self-monitor and self-evaluate language development

Goal 2: To use English to achieve academically in all content areas

Language Functions and Topics

Use contextual clues
Record observations
Rephrase, explain, revise, and expand information
Follow directions
Ask and answer questions
Express likes, dislikes, and needs
Gather and retell information
Represent information visually and interpret information presented visually
Connect new information to information previously learned

Goal 3: To use English in socially and culturally appropriate ways

Language Functions and Topics

Recognize irony, sarcasm, and humor
Use idiomatic speech
Respond to and use slang and idioms

ESL for Beginners, Volume One

Theme One: School — Day One Lesson

Objectives

The student will:

- Practice greeting and saying goodbye
- Practice saying the letters of the alphabet
- Practice saying the numbers 1–10
- Speak about *School* and understand *School* vocabulary
- Use the present-tense *to be* verb forms in a chant
- Use singular and plural pronouns correctly in sentences

Materials

- Appendices C/D/E/F/H/I/L, chart paper, vocabulary cards, alphabet cards, number cards, prizes, markers, and a ball

Activities with Informal Evaluations

The description/procedure for each activity below is in its appendix.

- Start the lesson with Circle Time, where the teacher greets each student, the class reads the day's date/activities together in English, and a student translates so everyone can understand the lesson's activities.
- Next, do the *School* vocabulary card warm-up (Appendix C).
- Do the alphabet/number card reviews (Appendices D and E) with students.
- Teach students the "To Be" chant (Appendix F).
- Teach the pronouns structure (Appendix L).
- Finally, meet back in a circle for the Circle Speaking Activity (Appendix H).
- End the lesson on a fun note with a game where students can win a prize. See Appendix I for a list/description of games. Numbers Bingo works well with this lesson.
- Say goodbye to students individually and have them respond.

Theme One: School — Day Two Lesson

Objectives

The student will:

- Practice greeting and saying goodbye
- Practice saying the letters of the alphabet
- Practice saying the numbers 1–10
- Speak about *School* and understand *School* vocabulary
- Use *to be* verbs in affirmative statements
- Use the question word *what* to gain information

Materials

- Appendices C/D/E/F/H/I/L, chart paper, vocabulary cards, alphabet cards, number cards, prizes, markers, and a ball

Activities with Informal Evaluations

The description/procedure for each activity below is in its appendix.

- Start the lesson with Circle Time, where the teacher greets each student, the class reads the day's date/activities together in English, and a student translates so everyone can understand the lesson's activities.
- Next, do the *School* vocabulary card warm-up (Appendix C).
- Do the alphabet/number card reviews (Appendices D and E) with students.
- Sing the "To Be" chant (Appendix F) with the class.
- Teach students the *to be* structure for affirmative statements (Appendix L).
- Introduce the class to the W & H Questions structure and then teach students how to use the question word *what* (Appendix L).
- Finally, meet back in a circle for the Circle Speaking Activity (Appendix H).
- End the lesson on a fun note with a game where students can win a prize. See Appendix I for a list/description of games. Numbers Bingo works well with this lesson.
- Say goodbye to students individually and have them respond.

Theme One: School — Day Three Lesson

Objectives

The student will:

- Practice greeting and saying goodbye
- Practice saying the letters of the alphabet
- Practice saying the numbers 1–10
- Speak about *School* and understand *School* vocabulary
- Use *to be* verbs in affirmative statements and questions
- Use *to be* verbs in a dialogue

Materials

- Appendices C/D/E/F/H/I/L/O, chart paper, vocabulary cards, alphabet cards, number cards, prizes, markers, and a ball

Activities with Informal Evaluations

The description/procedure for each activity below is in its appendix.

- Start the lesson with Circle Time, where the teacher greets each student, the class reads the day's date/activities together in English, and a student translates so everyone can understand the lesson's activities.
- Next, do the *School* vocabulary card warm-up (Appendix C).
- Do the alphabet/number card reviews (Appendices D and E) with students.
- Sing the "To Be" chant (Appendix F) with the class.
- Briefly review the *to be* structure for affirmative statements and then teach students the *to be* structure for questions (Appendix L).
- Complete the "To Be" dialogue (Appendix O, Dialogue #1) with students.
- Finally, meet back in a circle for the Circle Speaking Activity (Appendix H).
- End the lesson on a fun note with a game where students can win a prize. See Appendix I for a list/description of games. Alphabet Bingo works well with this lesson.
- Say goodbye to students individually and have them respond.

Theme One: School — Day Four Lesson

Objectives

The student will:

- Practice greeting and saying goodbye
- Practice saying the letters of the alphabet
- Practice saying the numbers 1–10
- Speak about *School* and understand *School* vocabulary
- Use *to be* verbs in statements and questions
- Use *to be* verbs in a dialogue about greetings

Materials

- Appendices C/D/E/F/H/I/L/O, chart paper, vocabulary cards, alphabet cards, number cards, prizes, markers, and a ball

Activities with Informal Evaluations

The description/procedure for each activity below is in its appendix.

- Start the lesson with Circle Time, where the teacher greets each student, the class reads the day's date/activities together in English, and a student translates so everyone can understand the lesson's activities.
- Next, do the *School* vocabulary card warm-up (Appendix C).
- Do the alphabet/number card reviews (Appendices D and E) with students.
- Sing the "To Be" chant (Appendix F) with the class.
- Briefly review the *to be* structure for affirmative statements and questions and then teach students the *to be* structure for negative statements (Appendix L).
- Complete the "Greetings" dialogue (Appendix O, Dialogue #2) with students.
- Finally, meet back in a circle for the Circle Speaking Activity (Appendix H).
- End the lesson on a fun note with a game where students can win a prize. See Appendix I for a list/description of games. Alphabet Bingo works well with this lesson.
- Say goodbye to students individually and have them respond.

Theme One: School — Day Five Lesson

Objectives

The student will:

- Practice greeting and saying goodbye
- Practice saying the letters of the alphabet
- Practice saying the numbers 1–10
- Speak about *School* and understand *School* vocabulary
- Use the *to be* verb forms in a chant
- Listen to and understand a short story
- Use W questions (*what*, *why*, *when*, *where*, *who*) to gain information

Materials

- Appendices C/D/E/F/G/H/I/L, chart paper, vocabulary cards, alphabet cards, number cards, prizes, markers, and sticky notes

Activities with Informal Evaluations

The description/procedure for each activity below is in its appendix.

- Start the lesson with Circle Time, where the teacher greets each student, the class reads the day's date/activities together in English, and a student translates so everyone can understand the lesson's activities.
- Next, do the *School* vocabulary card warm-up (Appendix C).
- Do the alphabet/number card reviews (Appendices D and E) with students.
- Sing the "To Be" chant (Appendix F) with the class.
- Teach students how to use the question words *why*, *when*, and *where* from the W & H Questions structure (Appendix L).
- Read and answer questions to Short Story #1 (Appendix G) with the class.
- Finally, meet back in a circle for the Circle Speaking Activity (Appendix H).
- End the lesson on a fun note with a game where students can win a prize. See Appendix I for a list/description of games. Play the "Name It!" game in this lesson, using the *School* vocabulary cards that the class has been practicing all week.
- Say goodbye to students individually and have them respond.

Theme Two: Home — Day One Lesson

Objectives

The student will:

- Practice greeting and saying goodbye
- Practice saying the letters of the alphabet and sing the "Alphabet Song"
- Practice saying the numbers 11–20
- Speak about *Home* and understand *Home* vocabulary
- Use the verb *can* in affirmative statements

Materials

- Appendices C/D/E/F/H/I/L, chart paper, vocabulary cards, alphabet cards, number cards, prizes, markers, and a ball

Activities with Informal Evaluations

The description/procedure for each activity below is in its appendix.

- Start the lesson with Circle Time, where the teacher greets each student, the class reads the day's date/activities together in English, and a student translates so everyone can understand the lesson's activities.
- Next, do the *Home* and *School* vocabulary card warm-up (Appendix C).
- Do the alphabet/number card reviews (Appendices D and E) with students.
- Teach students the "Alphabet Song" (Appendix F).
- Teach students the *can* structure for affirmative statements (Appendix L).
- Finally, meet back in a circle for the Circle Speaking Activity (Appendix H).
- End the lesson on a fun note with a game where students can win a prize. See Appendix I for a list/description of games. Numbers Bingo works well with this lesson.
- Say goodbye to students individually and have them respond.

Theme Two: Home — Day Two Lesson

Objectives

The student will:

- Practice greeting and saying goodbye
- Practice saying the letters of the alphabet and spell out his or her name orally
- Practice saying the numbers 11–20
- Speak about *Home* and understand *Home* vocabulary
- Use the verb *can* in affirmative and negative statements

Materials

- Appendices C/D/E/F/H/I/L, chart paper, vocabulary cards, alphabet cards, number cards, prizes, markers, and a ball

Activities with Informal Evaluations

The description/procedure for each activity below is in its appendix.

- Start the lesson with Circle Time, where the teacher greets each student, the class reads the day's date/activities together in English, and a student translates so everyone can understand the lesson's activities.
- Next, do the *Home* and *School* vocabulary card warm-up (Appendix C).
- Do the alphabet/number card reviews (Appendices D and E) with students.
- Sing the "Alphabet Song" (Appendix F) with the class.
- Have students do the "Spell Your Name" activity (Appendix H).
- Briefly review the *can* structure for affirmative statements and then teach students the *can* structure for negative statements (Appendix L).
- Finally, meet back in a circle for the Circle Speaking Activity (Appendix H).
- End the lesson on a fun note with a game where students can win a prize. See Appendix I for a list/description of games. Numbers Bingo works well with this lesson.
- Say goodbye to students individually and have them respond.

Theme Two: Home — Day Three Lesson

Objectives

The student will:

- Practice greeting and saying goodbye
- Practice saying the letters of the alphabet
- Practice saying the numbers 11–20
- Speak about *Home* and understand *Home* vocabulary
- Use the verb *can* in statements and questions

Materials

- Appendices C/D/E/F/H/I/L, chart paper, vocabulary cards, alphabet cards, number cards, prizes, markers, and a ball

Activities with Informal Evaluations

The description/procedure for each activity below is in its appendix.

- Start the lesson with Circle Time, where the teacher greets each student, the class reads the day's date/activities together in English, and a student translates so everyone can understand the lesson's activities.
- Next, do the *Home* and *School* vocabulary card warm-up (Appendix C).
- Do the alphabet/number card reviews (Appendices D and E) with students.
- Sing the "Alphabet Song" and/or the "To Be" chant (Appendix F) with the class.
- Briefly review the *can* structure for affirmative and negative statements and then teach students the *can* structure for questions (Appendix L).
- Finally, meet back in a circle for the Circle Speaking Activity (Appendix H).
- End the lesson on a fun note with a game where students can win a prize. See Appendix I for a list/description of games. Alphabet Bingo works well with this lesson.
- Say goodbye to students individually and have them respond.

Theme Two: Home — Day Four Lesson

Objectives

The student will:

- Practice greeting and saying goodbye
- Practice saying the letters of the alphabet
- Practice saying the numbers 11–20
- Speak about *Home* and understand *Home* vocabulary
- Orally answer short-story comprehension questions
- Use the question words outlined in the W & H Questions structure to gain information

Materials

- Appendices C/D/E/F/G/H/I/L, chart paper, vocabulary cards, alphabet cards, number cards, prizes, and markers

Activities with Informal Evaluations

The description/procedure for each activity below is in its appendix.

- Start the lesson with Circle Time, where the teacher greets each student, the class reads the day's date/activities together in English, and a student translates so everyone can understand the lesson's activities.
- Next, do the *Home* and *School* vocabulary card warm-up (Appendix C).
- Do the alphabet/number card reviews (Appendices D and E) with students.
- Sing the "Alphabet Song" and/or the "To Be" chant (Appendix F) with the class.
- Teach students how to use the question words *who*, *how, and how old* from the W & H Questions structure (Appendix L).
- Read and answer questions to Short Story #2 (Appendix G) with the class.
- Finally, meet back in a circle for the Circle Speaking Activity (Appendix H).
- End the lesson on a fun note with a game where students can win a prize. See Appendix I for a list/description of games. The "Simon Says" game works well with this lesson.
- Say goodbye to students individually and have them respond.

Theme Two: Home — Day Five Lesson

Objectives

The student will:

- Practice greeting and saying goodbye
- Practice saying the letters of the alphabet
- Practice saying the numbers 11–20
- Speak about *Home* and understand *Home* vocabulary
- Express not understanding with common phrases

Materials

- Appendices C/D/E/F/H/I, chart paper, vocabulary cards, alphabet cards, number cards, prizes, markers, and sticky notes

Activities with Informal Evaluations

The description/procedure for each activity below is in its appendix.

- Start the lesson with Circle Time, where the teacher greets each student, the class reads the day's date/activities together in English, and a student translates so everyone can understand the lesson's activities.
- Next, do the *Home* and *School* vocabulary card warm-up (Appendix C).
- Do the alphabet/number card reviews (Appendices D and E) with students.
- Sing the "Alphabet Song" and/or the "To Be" chant (Appendix F) with the class.
- Write each of the following phrases on chart paper and follow the same steps used to introduce the day's activities. Then give each student a chance to say the phrases in response to a statement he/she does not understand.
  - I do not know.
  - I do not understand.
  - I cannot.
- Finally, meet back in a circle for the Circle Speaking Activity (Appendix H).
- End the lesson on a fun note with a game where students can win a prize. See Appendix I for a list/description of games. Use the *School* and *Home* vocabulary cards to play the "Name It!" game with this lesson.
- Say goodbye to students individually and have them respond.

Theme Three: Nature — Day One Lesson

Objectives

The student will:

- Practice greeting and saying goodbye
- Practice saying the letters of the alphabet
- Practice saying the numbers to 11–20
- Speak about *Nature* and understand *Nature* vocabulary
- Use a TPR game to show the difference between the demonstrative words *this*, *that*, *these*, and *those*

Materials

- Appendices C/D/E/F/H/I/L, chart paper, vocabulary cards, alphabet cards, number cards, prizes, markers, and a ball

Activities with Informal Evaluations

The description/procedure for each activity below is in its appendix.

- Start the lesson with Circle Time, where the teacher greets each student, the class reads the day's date/activities together in English, and a student translates so everyone can understand the lesson's activities.
- Next, do the *Nature*, *Home*, and *School* vocabulary card warm-up (Appendix C).
- Do the alphabet/number card reviews (Appendices D and E) with students.
- Sing the "Alphabet Song" and the "To Be" chant (Appendix F).
- Teach students the demonstratives structure (Appendix L).
- Finally, meet back in a circle for the Circle Speaking Activity (Appendix H).
- End the lesson with the "This and That" game (Appendix I) where students can win a prize.
- Say goodbye to students individually and have them respond.

Theme Three: Nature — Day Two Lesson

Objectives

The student will:

- Practice greeting and saying goodbye
- Practice saying the letters of the alphabet
- Practice saying the numbers 11–20
- Speak about *Nature* and understand *Nature* vocabulary
- Use the *to do* verb in affirmative statements
- Learn and sing a song about demonstratives

Materials

- Appendices C/D/E/F/I/L, chart paper, vocabulary cards, alphabet cards, number cards, prizes, markers, and a ball

Activities with Informal Evaluations

The description/procedure for each activity below is in its appendix.

- Start the lesson with Circle Time, where the teacher greets each student, the class reads the day's date/activities together in English, and a student translates so everyone can understand the lesson's activities.
- Next, do the *Nature*, *Home*, and *School* vocabulary card warm-up (Appendix C).
- Do the alphabet/number card reviews (Appendices D and E) with students.
- Teach the class the "This and That" chant (Appendix F). Sing the "Alphabet Song" and the "To Be" chant with students.
- Teach students the *to do* structure for affirmative statements (Appendix L).
- End the lesson on a fun note with a game where students can win a prize. See Appendix I for a list/description of games. The "This/That/These/Those" game works well with this lesson.
- Say goodbye to students individually and have them respond.

Theme Three: Nature — Day Three Lesson

Objectives

The student will:

- Practice greeting and saying goodbye
- Practice saying the letters of the alphabet
- Practice saying the numbers 11–20
- Speak about *Nature* and understand *Nature* vocabulary
- Use the *to do* verb in affirmative and negative statements
- Use demonstratives to present a dialogue

Materials

- Appendices C/D/E/F/H/I/L/O, chart paper, vocabulary cards, alphabet cards, number cards, prizes, markers, and a ball

Activities with Informal Evaluations

The description/procedure for each activity below is in its appendix.

- Start the lesson with Circle Time, where the teacher greets each student, the class reads the day's date/activities together in English, and a student translates so everyone can understand the lesson's activities.
- Next, do the *Nature*, *Home*, and *School* vocabulary card warm-up (Appendix C).
- Do the alphabet/number card reviews (Appendices D and E) with students.
- Sing all the songs that the students have learned in this class (Appendix F).
- Briefly review the *to do* structure for affirmative statements and then teach students the *to do* structure for negative statements (Appendix L).
- Complete the "Demonstratives" dialogue (Appendix O, Dialogue #4) with students.
- Finally, meet back in a circle for the Circle Speaking Activity (Appendix H).
- End the lesson on a fun note with a game where students can win a prize. See Appendix I for a list/description of games. The "This/That/These/Those" game will work well with this lesson again.
- Say goodbye to students individually and have them respond.

Theme Three: Nature — Day Four Lesson

Objectives

The student will:

- Practice greeting and saying goodbye
- Practice saying the letters of the alphabet
- Practice saying the numbers 11–20
- Speak about *Nature* and understand *Nature* vocabulary
- Use affirmative, negative, and questions forms of the *to do* verb in statements
- Use the *can* verb to present a dialogue

Materials

- Appendices C/D/E/F/H/I/L/O, chart paper, vocabulary cards, alphabet cards, number cards, prizes, markers, and a ball

Activities with Informal Evaluations

The description/procedure for each activity below is in its appendix.

- Start the lesson with Circle Time, where the teacher greets each student, the class reads the day's date/activities together in English, and a student translates so everyone can understand the lesson's activities.
- Next, do the *Nature*, *Home*, and *School* vocabulary card warm-up (Appendix C).
- Do the alphabet/number card reviews (Appendices D and E) with students.
- Sing any or all of the songs/chants learned (Appendix F) with the class.
- Briefly review the *to do* structure for affirmative and negative statements and then teach students the *to do* structure for questions (Appendix L).
- Complete the "Can I?" dialogue (Appendix O, Dialogue #3) with students.
- Finally, meet back in a circle for the Circle Speaking Activity (Appendix H).
- End the lesson on a fun note with a game where students can win a prize. See Appendix I for a list/description of games. Alphabet Bingo works well with this lesson.
- Say goodbye to students individually and have them respond.

Theme Three: Nature — Day Five Lesson

Objectives

The student will:

- Practice greeting and saying goodbye
- Practice saying the letters of the alphabet
- Practice saying the numbers 11–20
- Speak about the *Nature* and understand *Nature* vocabulary
- Orally answer short-story comprehension questions

Materials

- Appendices C/D/E/F/G/H/I, chart paper, vocabulary cards, alphabet cards, number cards, prizes, markers, and sticky notes

Activities with Informal Evaluations

The description/procedure for each activity below is in its appendix.

- Start the lesson with Circle Time, where the teacher greets each student, the class reads the day's date/activities together in English, and a student translates so everyone can understand the lesson's activities.
- Next, do the *Nature*, *Home*, and *School* vocabulary card warm-up (Appendix C).
- Do the alphabet/number card reviews (Appendices D and E) with students.
- Sing any or all of the songs/chants learned so far (Appendix F) with the class.
- Read and answer questions to Short Story #3 (Appendix G) with the class.
- Finally, meet back in a circle for the Circle Speaking Activity (Appendix H).
- End the lesson on a fun note with a game where students can win a prize. See Appendix I for a list/description of games. Use the *Home*, *Nature*, and *School* vocabulary cards to play the "Name It!" game in this lesson.
- Say goodbye to students individually and have them respond.

Theme Four: Personal Hygiene — Day One Lesson

Objectives

The student will:

- Practice greeting and saying goodbye
- Practice saying the letters of the alphabet
- Speak about *Personal Hygiene* and understand *Personal Hygiene* vocabulary
- Use present-tense verbs in affirmative statements
- Review pronunciation/meaning of numbers to 1–20

Materials

- Appendices C/D/E/F/H/I/L, chart paper, vocabulary cards, alphabet cards, number cards, prizes, markers, and a ball

Activities with Informal Evaluations

The description/procedure for each activity below is in its appendix.

- Start the lesson with Circle Time, where the teacher greets each student, the class reads the day's date/activities together in English, and a student translates so everyone can understand the lesson's activities.
- Next, do the *Personal Hygiene*, *Nature*, *Home*, and *School* vocabulary card warm-up (Appendix C).
- Do the alphabet/number card reviews (Appendices D and E) with students.
- Sing any or all of the songs/chants learned (Appendix F) with the class.
- Teach students the present-tense structure for affirmative statements (Appendix L).
- Finally, meet back in a circle for the Circle Speaking Activity (Appendix H).
- End the lesson on a fun note with a game where students can win a prize. See Appendix I for a list/description of games. Numbers Bingo works well with this lesson.
- Say goodbye to students individually and have them respond.

Theme Four: Personal Hygiene — Day Two Lesson

Objectives

The student will:

- Practice greeting and saying goodbye
- Practice saying the letters of the alphabet
- Speak about *Personal Hygiene* and understand *Personal Hygiene* vocabulary
- Sing a song about personal hygiene
- Use present-tense verbs in affirmative and negative statements
- Review pronunciation/meaning of numbers to 1–20

Materials

- Appendices C/D/E/F/H/I/L, chart paper, vocabulary cards, alphabet cards, number cards, prizes, markers, and a ball

Activities with Informal Evaluations

The description/procedure for each activity below is in its appendix.

- Start the lesson with Circle Time, where the teacher greets each student, the class reads the day's date/activities together in English, and a student translates so everyone can understand the lesson's activities.
- Next, do the *Personal Hygiene*, *Nature*, *Home*, and *School* vocabulary card warm-up (Appendix C).
- Do the alphabet/number card reviews (Appendices D and E) with students.
- Teach students the "This Is the Way" song (Appendix F). If there is time, sing the other songs that the class has learned.
- Briefly review the present-tense structure for affirmative statements. Teach students the present-tense structure for negative statements (Appendix L).
- Finally, meet back in a circle for the Circle Speaking Activity (Appendix H).
- End the lesson on a fun note with a game where students can win a prize. See Appendix I for a list/description of games. Alphabet Bingo works well with this lesson.
- Say goodbye to students individually and have them respond.

Theme Four: Personal Hygiene — Day Three Lesson

Objectives

The student will:

- Practice greeting and saying goodbye
- Practice saying the letters of the alphabet
- Speak about *Personal Hygiene* and understand *Personal Hygiene* vocabulary
- Practice speaking about numbers and birthdays in a dialogue
- Practice using verbs in the present tense
- Review pronunciation/meaning of numbers to 1–20

Materials

- Appendices C/D/E/F/H/I/L/O, chart paper, vocabulary cards, alphabet cards, number cards, prizes, markers, and a ball

Activities with Informal Evaluations

The description/procedure for each activity below is in its appendix.

- Start the lesson with Circle Time, where the teacher greets each student, the class reads the day's date/activities together in English, and a student translates so everyone can understand the lesson's activities.
- Next, do the *Personal Hygiene*, *Nature*, *Home*, and *School* vocabulary card warm-up (Appendix C).
- Do the alphabet/number card reviews (Appendices D and E) with students.
- Sing all songs learned (Appendix F) with the class.
- Complete the "Numbers/Birthday" dialogue (Appendix O, Dialogue #5) with students.
- Briefly review the present-tense structure for affirmative and negative statements. Teach students the present-tense structure for questions (Appendix L).
- Finally, meet back in a circle for the Circle Speaking Activity (Appendix H).
- End the lesson on a fun note with a game where students can win a prize. See Appendix I for a list/description of games. The "This/That/These/Those" game works well with this lesson.
- Say goodbye to students individually and have them respond.

Theme Four: Personal Hygiene — Day Four Lesson

Objectives

The student will:

- Practice greeting and saying goodbye
- Practice saying the letters of the alphabet
- Speak about *Personal Hygiene* and understand *Personal Hygiene* vocabulary
- Orally answer short-story comprehension questions
- Review pronunciation/meaning of numbers to 1–20

Materials

- Appendices C/D/E/F/G/H/I, chart paper, vocabulary cards, alphabet cards, number cards, prizes, and markers

Activities with Informal Evaluations

The description/procedure for each activity below is in its appendix.

- Start the lesson with Circle Time, where the teacher greets each student, the class reads the day's date/activities together in English, and a student translates so everyone can understand the lesson's activities.
- Next, do the *Personal Hygiene*, *Nature*, *Home*, and *School* vocabulary card warm-up (Appendix C).
- Do the alphabet/number card reviews (Appendices D and E) with students.
- Sing all songs learned (Appendix F) with the class.
- Read and answer questions to Short Story #4 (Appendix G) with the class. If there is time, do an Observation Walk (Appendix H) with the class.
- Finally, meet back in a circle for the Circle Speaking Activity (Appendix H).
- End the lesson on a fun note with a game where students can win a prize. See Appendix I for a list/description of games. The "Simon Says" game or Alphabet Bingo works well with this lesson.
- Say goodbye to students individually and have them respond.

Theme Four: Personal Hygiene — Day Five Lesson

Objectives

The student will:

- Practice greeting and saying goodbye
- Practice saying the letters of the alphabet
- Write and read a class story using the topics and structures learned in this volume
- Speak about *Personal Hygiene* and understand *Personal Hygiene* vocabulary
- Review pronunciation/meaning of numbers to 1–20

Materials

- Appendices C/D/E/F/H/I, chart paper, vocabulary cards, alphabet cards, number cards, prizes, and sticky notes

Activities with Informal Evaluations

The description/procedure for each activity below is in its appendix.

- Start the lesson with Circle Time, where the teacher greets each student, the class reads the day's date/activities together in English, and a student translates so everyone can understand the lesson's activities.
- Next, do the *Personal Hygiene*, *Nature*, *Home*, and *School* vocabulary card warm-up (Appendix C).
- Do the alphabet/number card reviews (Appendices D and E) with students.
- Sing all songs learned (Appendix F) with the class.
- Complete a Language Experience Activity (Appendix H) with the class.
- Finally, meet back in a circle for the Circle Speaking Activity (Appendix H).
- End the lesson on a fun note with a game where students can win a prize. See Appendix I for a list/description of games. Use all of this volume's vocabulary cards to play the "Name It!" game in this lesson.
- Say goodbye to students individually and have them respond.

ESL for Beginners, Volume Two

Theme Five: The Body — Day One Lesson

Objectives

The student will:

- Practice greeting and saying goodbye
- Practice saying the letters of the alphabet
- Practice saying the numbers 20–30
- Speak about *The Body* and understand *The Body* vocabulary
- Review the present-tense verb structure with a chant
- Listen to and understand a chapter book as it is read aloud
- Orally answer comprehension questions about the chapter book

Materials

- Appendices C/D/E/F/I/Q, chart paper, vocabulary cards, alphabet cards, number cards, prizes, markers, and a read-aloud chapter book

Activities with Informal Evaluations

The description/procedure for each activity below is in its appendix.

- Start the lesson with Circle Time, where the teacher greets each student, the class reads the day's date/activities together in English, and a student translates so everyone can understand the lesson's activities.
- Next, do the *The Body* vocabulary card warm-up (Appendix C) and mix in some vocabulary cards from the previous four themes.
- Do the alphabet/number card reviews (Appendices D and E) with students.
- Start reading the chapter book aloud and then ask each student one comprehension question (Appendix Q).
- Teach students the "Present-Tense" chant (Appendix F).
- Play a game of your choice (Appendix I) and sing a few songs (Appendix F) with the class.
- Say goodbye to students individually and have them respond.

Theme Five: The Body — Day Two Lesson

Objectives

The student will:

- Practice greeting and saying goodbye
- Practice saying the letters of the alphabet
- Practice saying the numbers 20–30
- Speak about *The Body* and understand *The Body* vocabulary
- Review present-tense verbs in a new game
- Listen to and understand a chapter book as it is read aloud
- Orally answer comprehension questions about the chapter book

Materials

- Appendices C/D/E/F/I/L/Q, chart paper, vocabulary cards, alphabet cards, number cards, prizes, markers, a read-aloud chapter book, and a ball

Activities with Informal Evaluations

The description/procedure for each activity below is in its appendix.

- Start the lesson with Circle Time, where the teacher greets each student, the class reads the day's date/activities together in English, and a student translates so everyone can understand the lesson's activities.
- Next, do the *The Body* vocabulary card warm-up (Appendix C) and mix in some vocabulary cards from the previous four themes.
- Do the alphabet/number card reviews (Appendices D and E) with students.
- Continue reading the chapter book aloud and then ask each student one comprehension question (Appendix Q).
- Review the present-tense verb structure (Appendix L) and play the "Pick the Right Verb!" game (Appendix I) with the class.
- Sing a few songs (Appendix F) with the class.
- Say goodbye to students individually and have them respond.

Theme Five: The Body — Day Three Lesson

Objectives

The student will:

- Practice greeting and saying goodbye
- Practice saying the letters of the alphabet
- Practice saying the numbers 20–30
- Speak about *The Body* and understand *The Body* vocabulary
- Use possessive adjectives correctly in statements and questions
- Listen to and understand a chapter book as it is read aloud
- Orally answer comprehension questions about the chapter book

Materials

- Appendices C/D/E/F/I/L/Q, chart paper, vocabulary cards, alphabet cards, number cards, prizes, markers, a read-aloud chapter book, and a ball

Activities with Informal Evaluations

The description/procedure for each activity below is in its appendix.

- Start the lesson with Circle Time, where the teacher greets each student, the class reads the day's date/activities together in English, and a student translates so everyone can understand the lesson's activities.
- Next, do *The Body* vocabulary card warm-up (Appendix C) and mix in some vocabulary cards from the previous four themes.
- Do the alphabet/number card reviews (Appendices D and E) with students.
- Continue reading the chapter book aloud and then ask each student one comprehension question (Appendix Q).
- Teach students the possessive adjectives structure (Appendix L).
- Play a game of your choice (Appendix I) and sing a few songs (Appendix F) with the class.
- Say goodbye to students individually and have them respond.

Theme Five: The Body — Day Four Lesson

Objectives

The student will:

- Practice greeting and saying goodbye
- Practice saying the letters of the alphabet
- Practice saying the numbers 20–30
- Speak about *The Body* and understand *The Body* vocabulary
- Use *The Body* vocabulary in a "Word Splash!" activity
- Listen to and understand a chapter book as it is read aloud
- Orally answer comprehension questions about the chapter book

Materials

- Appendices C/D/E/F/H/I/Q, chart paper, vocabulary cards, alphabet cards, number cards, prizes, markers, and a read-aloud chapter book

Activities with Informal Evaluations

The description/procedure for each activity below is in its appendix.

- Start the lesson with Circle Time, where the teacher greets each student, the class reads the day's date/activities together in English, and a student translates so everyone can understand the lesson's activities.
- Next, do the *The Body* vocabulary card warm-up (Appendix C) and mix in some vocabulary cards from the previous four themes.
- Do the alphabet/number card reviews (Appendices D and E) with students.
- Continue reading the chapter book aloud and then ask each student one comprehension question (Appendix Q).
- Do the "Word Splash!" activity (Appendix H) with the class.
- Play a game of your choice (Appendix I) and sing a few songs (Appendix F) with the class.
- Say goodbye to students individually and have them respond.

Theme Five: The Body — Day Five Lesson

Objectives

The student will:

- Practice greeting and saying goodbye
- Practice saying the letters of the alphabet
- Practice saying the numbers 20–30
- Speak about *The Body* and understand *The Body* vocabulary
- Review the present-tense verb structure to complete a Language Experience Activity
- Listen to and understand a chapter book as it is read aloud
- Orally answer comprehension questions about the chapter book

Materials

- Appendices C/D/E/F/H/I/Q, chart paper, vocabulary cards, alphabet cards, number cards, prizes, markers, and a read-aloud chapter book

Activities with Informal Evaluations

The description/procedure for each activity below is in its appendix.

- Start the lesson with Circle Time, where the teacher greets each student, the class reads the day's date/activities together in English, and a student translates so everyone can understand the lesson's activities.
- Next, do the *The Body* vocabulary card warm-up (Appendix C) and mix in some vocabulary cards from the previous four themes.
- Do the alphabet/number card reviews (Appendices D and E) with students.
- Continue reading the chapter book aloud and then ask each student one comprehension question (Appendix Q).
- Use *The Body* vocabulary (Appendix C) to do the Language Experience Activity (Appendix H) with the class.
- Play a game of your choice (Appendix I) and sing a few songs (Appendix F) with the class.
- Say goodbye to students individually and have them respond.

Theme Six: Occupations — Day One Lesson

Objectives

The student will:

- Practice greeting and saying goodbye
- Practice saying the letters of the alphabet
- Practice saying the numbers 20–40
- Speak about *Occupations* and understand *Occupations* vocabulary
- Listen to and understand a chapter book as it is read aloud
- Orally answer comprehension questions about the chapter book
- Use the irregular verb *to go* in affirmative present-tense statements

Materials

- Appendices C/D/E/F/I/L/Q, chart paper, vocabulary cards, alphabet cards, number cards, prizes, markers, a read-aloud chapter book, and a ball

Activities with Informal Evaluations

The description/procedure for each activity below is in its appendix.

- Start the lesson with Circle Time, where the teacher greets each student, the class reads the day's date/activities together in English, and a student translates so everyone can understand the lesson's activities.
- Next, do the *Occupations* vocabulary card warm-up (Appendix C) and mix in some vocabulary cards from the previous five themes.
- Do the alphabet/number card reviews (Appendices D and E) with students.
- Continue reading the chapter book aloud and then ask each student one comprehension question (Appendix Q).
- Teach the *to go* affirmative structure (Appendix L) to the class.
- Play a game of your choice (Appendix I) and sing a few songs (Appendix F) with the class.
- Say goodbye to students individually and have them respond.

Theme Six: Occupations — Day Two Lesson

Objectives

The student will:

- Practice greeting and saying goodbye
- Practice saying the letters of the alphabet
- Practice saying the numbers 20–40
- Speak about *Occupations* and understand *Occupations* vocabulary
- Listen to and understand a chapter book as it is read aloud
- Orally answer comprehension questions about the chapter book
- Use vocabulary for days of the week in a song
- Use the *to go* verb in present-tense negative statements

Materials

- Appendices C/D/E/F/L/Q, chart paper, vocabulary cards, alphabet cards, number cards, prizes, markers, a read-aloud chapter book, and a ball

Activities with Informal Evaluations

The description/procedure for each activity below is in its appendix.

- Start the lesson with Circle Time, where the teacher greets each student, the class reads the day's date/activities together in English, and a student translates so everyone can understand the lesson's activities.
- Next, do the *Occupations* vocabulary card warm-up (Appendix C) and mix in some vocabulary cards from the previous five themes.
- Do the alphabet/number card reviews (Appendices D and E) with students.
- Continue reading the chapter book aloud and then ask each student one comprehension question (Appendix Q).
- Briefly review the *to go* structure for present-tense affirmative statements and then teach students the *to go* structure for present-tense negative statements (Appendix L).
- Teach the class the "Days of the Week" song (Appendix F) and sing it together.
- Say goodbye to students individually and have them respond.

Theme Six: Occupations — Day Three Lesson

Objectives

The student will:

- Practice greeting and saying goodbye
- Practice saying the letters of the alphabet
- Practice saying the numbers 20–40
- Speak about *Occupations* and understand *Occupations* vocabulary
- Listen to and understand a chapter book as it is read aloud
- Orally answer comprehension questions about the chapter book
- Use *to go* verbs in a conversation

Materials

- Appendices C/D/E/L/P/Q, chart paper, vocabulary cards, alphabet cards, number cards, prizes, markers, a read-aloud chapter book, and a ball

Activities with Informal Evaluations

The description/procedure for each activity below is in its appendix.

- Start the lesson with Circle Time, where the teacher greets each student, the class reads the day's date/activities together in English, and a student translates so everyone can understand the lesson's activities.
- Next, do the *Occupations* vocabulary card warm-up (Appendix C) and mix in some vocabulary cards from the previous five themes.
- Do the alphabet/number card reviews (Appendices D and E) with students.
- Read the chapter book aloud and then ask each student one comprehension question (Appendix Q).
- Briefly review the *to go* structure for present-tense affirmative and negative statements and then teach students the *to go* structure for present-tense questions (Appendix L).
- Have the students work in pairs to create, practice, and present Stem Conversation #2 (Appendix P).
- Say goodbye to students individually and have them respond.

Theme Six: Occupations — Day Four Lesson

Objectives

The student will:

- Practice greeting and saying goodbye
- Practice saying the letters of the alphabet
- Practice saying the numbers 20–40
- Speak about *Occupations* and understand *Occupations* vocabulary
- Use present-continuous verbs in affirmative statements
- Listen to and understand a chapter book as it is read aloud
- Orally answer comprehension questions about the chapter book

Materials

- Appendices C/D/E/F/I/L/Q, chart paper, vocabulary cards, alphabet cards, number cards, prizes, markers, a read-aloud chapter book, and a ball

Activities with Informal Evaluations

The description/procedure for each activity below is in its appendix.

- Start the lesson with Circle Time, where the teacher greets each student, the class reads the day's date/activities together in English, and a student translates so everyone can understand the lesson's activities.
- Next, do the *Occupations* vocabulary card warm-up (Appendix C) and mix in some vocabulary cards from the previous five themes.
- Do the alphabet/number card reviews (Appendices D and E) with students.
- Read the chapter book aloud and then ask each student one comprehension question (Appendix Q).
- Teach students the present-continuous verb structure for affirmative statements (Appendix L).
- Play a game of your choice (Appendix I) and sing a few songs (Appendix F) with the class.
- Say goodbye to students individually and have them respond.

Theme Six: Occupations — Day Five Lesson

Objectives

The student will:

- Practice greeting and saying goodbye
- Practice saying the letters of the alphabet
- Practice saying the numbers 20–40
- Speak about *Occupations* and understand *Occupations* vocabulary
- Use present-continuous verbs in affirmative and negative statements
- Listen to and understand a chapter book as it is read aloud
- Orally answer comprehension questions about the chapter book

Materials

- Appendices C/D/E/F/H/I/L/Q, chart paper, vocabulary cards, alphabet cards, number cards, prizes, markers, a read-aloud chapter book, and a ball

Activities with Informal Evaluations

The description/procedure for each activity below is in its appendix.

- Start the lesson with Circle Time, where the teacher greets each student, the class reads the day's date/activities together in English, and a student translates so everyone can understand the lesson's activities.
- Next, do the *Occupations* vocabulary card warm-up (Appendix C) and mix in some vocabulary cards from the previous five themes.
- Do the alphabet/number card reviews (Appendices D and E) with students.
- Continue reading the chapter book aloud and then ask each student one comprehension question (Appendix Q).
- Briefly review the present-continuous verb structure for affirmative statements and then teach students the present-continuous structure for negative statements (Appendix L).
- Do the "Guess It!" activity (Appendix H) with the class.
- If there is time, play a game of your choice (Appendix I) and sing a few songs (Appendix F) with the class.
- Say goodbye to students individually and have them respond.

Theme Seven: Technology — Day One Lesson

Objectives

The student will:

- Practice greeting and saying goodbye
- Practice saying the letters of the alphabet
- Practice saying the numbers 20–50
- Speak about *Technology* and understand *Technology* vocabulary
- Listen to and understand a chapter book as it is read aloud
- Orally answer comprehension questions about the chapter book
- Use present-continuous verbs in statements and questions

Materials

- Appendices C/D/E/H/L/Q, chart paper, vocabulary cards, alphabet cards, number cards, prizes, markers, a read-aloud chapter book, and a ball

Activities with Informal Evaluations

The description/procedure for each activity below is in its appendix.

- Start the lesson with Circle Time, where the teacher greets each student, the class reads the day's date/activities together in English, and a student translates so everyone can understand the lesson's activities.
- Next, do the *Technology* vocabulary card warm-up (Appendix C) and mix in some vocabulary cards from the previous six themes.
- Do the alphabet/number card reviews (Appendices D and E) with students.
- Continue reading the chapter book aloud and then ask each student one comprehension question (Appendix Q).
- Briefly review the present-continuous verb structure for affirmative and negative statements and then teach students the present-continuous structure for questions (Appendix L).
- Go on an Observation Walk (Appendix H) with the class.
- Say goodbye to students individually and have them respond.

Theme Seven: Technology — Day Two Lesson

Objectives

The student will:

- Practice greeting and saying goodbye
- Practice saying the letters of the alphabet
- Practice saying the numbers 20–50
- Speak about *Technology* and understand *Technology* vocabulary
- Listen to and understand a chapter book as it is read aloud
- Orally answer comprehension questions about the chapter book
- Use the *to have* verb in present-tense affirmative statements

Materials

- Appendices C/D/E/F/H/I/L/Q, chart paper, vocabulary cards, alphabet cards, number cards, prizes, markers, a read-aloud chapter book, drawing paper, and a ball

Activities with Informal Evaluations

The description/procedure for each activity below is in its appendix.

- Start the lesson with Circle Time, where the teacher greets each student, the class reads the day's date/activities together in English, and a student translates so everyone can understand the lesson's activities.
- Next, do the *Technology* vocabulary card warm-up (Appendix C) and mix in some vocabulary cards from the previous six themes.
- Do the alphabet/number card reviews (Appendices D and E) with students.
- Continue reading the chapter book aloud and then ask each student one comprehension question (Appendix Q).
- Teach students the *to have* present-tense structure for affirmative statements (Appendix L).
- Do the Quick Sketch Activity (Appendix H) with the class using the *Technology* vocabulary (Appendix C).
- If there is time, play a game of your choice (Appendix I) and sing a few songs (Appendix F) with the class.
- Say goodbye to students individually and have them respond.

Theme Seven: Technology — Day Three Lesson

Objectives

The student will:

- Practice greeting and saying goodbye
- Practice saying the letters of the alphabet
- Practice saying the numbers 20–50
- Speak about *Technology* and understand *Technology* vocabulary
- Listen to and understand a chapter book as it is read aloud
- Orally answer comprehension questions about the chapter book
- Use the *to have* verb correctly in present-tense affirmative and negative statements

Materials

- Appendices C/D/E/F/I/L/Q, chart paper, vocabulary cards, alphabet cards, number cards, prizes, markers, a read-aloud chapter book, and a ball

Activities with Informal Evaluations

The description/procedure for each activity below is in its appendix.

- Start the lesson with Circle Time, where the teacher greets each student, the class reads the day's date/activities together in English, and a student translates so everyone can understand the lesson's activities.
- Next, do the *Technology* vocabulary card warm-up (Appendix C) and mix in some vocabulary cards from the previous six themes.
- Do the alphabet/number card reviews (Appendices D and E) with students.
- Continue reading the chapter book aloud and then ask each student one comprehension question (Appendix Q).
- Briefly review the *to have* structure for present-tense affirmative statements and then teach students the *to have* structure for present-tense negative statements (Appendix L).
- Play a game of your choice (Appendix I) and sing a few songs (Appendix F) with the class.
- Say goodbye to students individually and have them respond.

Theme Seven: Technology — Day Four Lesson

Objectives

The student will:

- Practice greeting and saying goodbye
- Practice saying the letters of the alphabet
- Practice saying the numbers 20–50
- Speak about *Technology* and understand *Technology* vocabulary
- Listen to and understand a chapter book as it is read aloud
- Orally answer comprehension questions about the chapter book
- Use affirmative, negative, and question forms of the *to have* verb in a new song

Materials

- Appendices C/D/E/F/I/L/Q, chart paper, vocabulary cards, alphabet cards, number cards, prizes, markers, a read-aloud chapter book, and a ball

Activities with Informal Evaluations

The description/procedure for each activity below is in its appendix.

- Start the lesson with Circle Time, where the teacher greets each student, the class reads the day's date/activities together in English, and a student translates so everyone can understand the lesson's activities.
- Next, do the *Technology* vocabulary card warm-up (Appendix C) and mix in some vocabulary cards from the previous six themes.
- Do the alphabet/number card reviews (Appendices D and E) with students.
- Continue reading the chapter book aloud and then ask each student one comprehension question (Appendix Q).
- Briefly review the *to have* verb structure for present-tense affirmative and negative statements and then teach students the *to have* structure for questions (Appendix L).
- Teach the class the "Have You Seen the Ghost of John?" song (Appendix F) and sing it together.
- Play a game of your choice (Appendix I).
- Say goodbye to students individually and have them respond.

Theme Seven: Technology — Day Five Lesson

Objectives

The student will:

- Practice greeting and saying goodbye
- Practice saying the letters of the alphabet
- Practice saying the numbers 20–50
- Speak about *Technology* and understand *Technology* vocabulary
- Listen to and understand a chapter book as it is read aloud
- Orally answer comprehension questions about the chapter book
- Use the plurals structure correctly in a conversation

Materials

- Appendices C/D/E/F/I/L/P/Q, chart paper, vocabulary cards, alphabet cards, number cards, prizes, markers, a read-aloud chapter book, and a ball

Activities with Informal Evaluations

The description/procedure for each activity below is in its appendix.

- Start the lesson with Circle Time, where the teacher greets each student, the class reads the day's date/activities together in English, and a student translates so everyone can understand the lesson's activities.
- Next, do the *Technology* vocabulary card warm-up (Appendix C) and mix in some vocabulary cards from the previous six themes.
- Do the alphabet/number card reviews (Appendices D and E) with students.
- Continue reading the chapter book aloud and then ask each student one comprehension question (Appendix Q).
- Teach students the plurals structure (Appendix L).
- Have the students work in pairs to create, practice, and present Stem Conversation #1 (Appendix P).
- If there is time, play a game of your choice (Appendix I) and sing a few songs (Appendix F) with the class.
- Say goodbye to students individually and have them respond.

Theme Eight: Transportation — Day One Lesson

Objectives

The student will:

- Practice greeting and saying goodbye
- Practice saying the letters of the alphabet
- Practice saying the numbers 1–50
- Speak about *Transportation* and understand *Transportation* vocabulary
- Listen to and understand a chapter book as it is read aloud
- Orally answer comprehension questions about the chapter book
- Use the commands structure to speak/respond to commands and to show prepositions of location (*on, at, in*)

Materials

- Appendices C/D/E/F/I/L/Q, chart paper, vocabulary cards, alphabet cards, number cards, prizes, markers, a read-aloud chapter book, and a ball

Activities with Informal Evaluations

The description/procedure for each activity below is in its appendix.

- Start the lesson with Circle Time, where the teacher greets each student, the class reads the day's date/activities together in English, and a student translates so everyone can understand the lesson's activities.
- Next, do the *Transportation* vocabulary card warm-up (Appendix C) and mix in some vocabulary cards from the previous seven themes.
- Do the alphabet/number card reviews (Appendices D and E) with students.
- Read the chapter book aloud and then ask each student one comprehension question (Appendix Q).
- Teach students the commands structure (Appendix L) and prepositions of location (*on/at/in*).
- Play "Simon Says" (Appendix I) and sing a few songs (Appendix F) with the class.
- Say goodbye to students individually and have them respond.

Theme Eight: Transportation — Day Two Lesson

Objectives

The student will:

- Practice greeting and saying goodbye
- Practice saying the letters of the alphabet
- Practice saying the numbers 1–50
- Speak about *Transportation* and understand *Transportation* vocabulary
- Listen to and understand a chapter book as it is read aloud
- Orally answer comprehension questions about the chapter book
- Speak/respond to commands
- Show prepositions *on/at/in* with body movements

Materials

- Appendices C/D/E/F/H/I/Q, chart paper, vocabulary cards, alphabet cards, number cards, prizes, markers, and a read-aloud chapter book

Activities with Informal Evaluations

The description/procedure for each activity below is in its appendix.

- Start the lesson with Circle Time, where the teacher greets each student, the class reads the day's date/activities together in English, and a student translates so everyone can understand the lesson's activities.
- Next, do the *Transportation* vocabulary card warm-up (Appendix C) and mix in some vocabulary cards from the previous seven themes.
- Do the alphabet/number card reviews (Appendices D and E) with students.
- Continue reading the chapter book aloud and then ask each student one comprehension question (Appendix Q).
- Do the Kinesthetic Practice Activity in Appendix H with prepositions of location (*on/at/in*).
- Play a game of your choice (Appendix I) and sing a few songs (Appendix F) with the class.
- Say goodbye to students individually and have them respond.

Theme Eight: Transportation — Day Three Lesson

Objectives

The student will:

- Practice greeting and saying goodbye
- Practice saying the letters of the alphabet
- Practice saying the numbers 1–50
- Speak about *Transportation* and understand *Transportation* vocabulary
- Listen to and understand a chapter book as it is read aloud
- Orally answer comprehension questions about the chapter book
- Have a conversation about and respond to commands

Materials

- Appendices C/D/E/F/I/P/Q, chart paper, vocabulary cards, alphabet cards, number cards, prizes, markers, and a read-aloud chapter book

Activities with Informal Evaluations

The description/procedure for each activity below is in its appendix.

- Start the lesson with Circle Time, where the teacher greets each student, the class reads the day's date/activities together in English, and a student translates so everyone can understand the lesson's activities.
- Next, do the *Transportation* vocabulary card warm-up (Appendix C) and mix in some vocabulary cards from the previous seven themes.
- Do the alphabet/number card reviews (Appendices D and E) with students.
- Continue reading the chapter book aloud and then ask each student one comprehension question (Appendix Q).
- Have the students work in pairs to create, practice, and present Stem Conversation #3 (Appendix P).
- Play "Simon Says" (Appendix I) and sing a few songs (Appendix F) with the class.
- Say goodbye to students individually and have them respond.

Theme Eight: Transportation — Day Four Lesson

Objectives

The student will:

- Practice greeting and saying goodbye
- Practice saying the letters of the alphabet
- Practice saying the numbers 1–50
- Speak about *Transportation* and understand *Transportation* vocabulary
- Listen to and understand a chapter book as it is read aloud
- Orally answer comprehension questions about the chapter book
- Use letter names in a Spelling Bee

Materials

- Appendices C/D/E/F/H/I/Q, chart paper, vocabulary cards, alphabet cards, number cards, prizes, markers, a read-aloud chapter book, and Realia transportation objects to share

Activities with Informal Evaluations

The description/procedure for each activity below is in its appendix.

- Start the lesson with Circle Time, where the teacher greets each student, the class reads the day's date/activities together in English, and a student translates so everyone can understand the lesson's activities.
- Next, do the *Transportation* vocabulary card warm-up (Appendix C) and mix in some vocabulary cards from the previous seven themes.
- Do the alphabet/number card reviews (Appendices D and E) with students.
- Continue reading the chapter book aloud and then ask each student one comprehension question (Appendix Q).
- Using transportation objects, do the Realia Activity (Appendix H) with the class.
- Play "Spelling Bee" (Appendix I) using the transportation vocabulary cards (Appendix C).
- Say goodbye to students individually and have them respond.

Theme Eight: Transportation — Day Five Lesson

Objectives

The student will:

- Practice greeting and saying goodbye
- Practice saying the letters of the alphabet
- Practice saying the numbers 1–50
- Speak about *Transportation* and understand *Transportation* vocabulary
- Listen to and understand a chapter book as it is read aloud
- Orally answer comprehension questions about the chapter book
- Use letter names by spelling aloud his/her partner's name

Materials

- Appendices C/D/E/F/H/I, chart paper, vocabulary cards, alphabet cards, number cards, prizes, a read-aloud chapter book, and student Realia objects (see Appendix H for description of objects)

Activities with Informal Evaluations

The description/procedure for each activity below is in its appendix.

- Start the lesson with Circle Time, where the teacher greets each student, the class reads the day's date/activities together in English, and a student translates so everyone can understand the lesson's activities.
- Next, do the *Transportation* vocabulary card warm-up (Appendix C) and mix in some vocabulary cards from the previous seven themes.
- Do the alphabet/number card reviews (Appendices D and E) with students.
- Finish reading the chapter book aloud and then ask each student to share his or her favorite part of the story (Appendix Q).
- Using transportation objects, finish the Realia Activity (Appendix H) with the class.
- Do the "Spell Your Name" activity using the Partner Version (Appendix H).
- If there is time, play a game of your choice (Appendix I) and sing a few songs (Appendix F) with the class.
- Say goodbye to students individually and have them respond.

ESL for Beginners, Volume Three

Theme Nine: Feelings — Day One Lesson

Objectives

The student will:

- Practice greeting and saying goodbye
- Practice saying the letters of the alphabet
- Practice saying the numbers 50–60
- Speak about *Feelings* and understand *Feelings* vocabulary
- Review the present-tense *to be* verb structure
- Sing a song about past-tense *to be* verbs
- Listen to a chapter book as it is read aloud and orally answer comprehension questions
- Analyze and understand language in a short video clip

Materials

- Appendices C/D/E/F/H/K/L/Q, chart paper, vocabulary cards, alphabet cards, number cards, prizes, markers, a read-aloud chapter book, and a video clip to show with a computer or DVD player

Activities with Informal Evaluations

The description/procedure for each activity below is in its appendix.

- Start the lesson with Circle Time, where the teacher greets each student, the class reads the day's date/activities together in English, and a student translates so everyone can understand the lesson's activities.
- Next, do the *Feelings* vocabulary card warm-up (Appendix C) and mix in some vocabulary cards from the previous eight themes.
- Do the alphabet/number card reviews (Appendices D and E) with students.
- Start reading a new chapter book aloud and then ask each student one comprehension question (Appendix Q).
- Do the Video Clip Activity (Appendix H).
- Teach the "Past-Tense 'To Be'" chant (Appendix F) and review the present-tense *to be* structure (Appendix L).
- Play the word wall game, "You Can Act" (Appendix K) to review present-tense concepts.
- Say goodbye to students individually and have them respond.

Theme Nine: Feelings — Day Two Lesson

Objectives

The student will:

- Practice greeting and saying goodbye
- Practice saying the letters of the alphabet
- Practice saying the numbers 50–60
- Speak about *Feelings* and understand *Feelings* vocabulary
- Use past-tense *to be* verbs to make affirmative statements
- Listen to and understand a chapter book as it is read aloud
- Orally answer comprehension questions about the chapter book
- Analyze and understand language in a short video clip

Materials

- Appendices C/D/E/F/H/K/L/Q, chart paper, vocabulary cards, alphabet cards, number cards, prizes, markers, a read-aloud chapter book, a ball, and a video clip to show with a computer or DVD player

Activities with Informal Evaluations

The description/procedure for each activity below is in its appendix.

- Start the lesson with Circle Time, where the teacher greets each student, the class reads the day's date/activities together in English, and a student translates so everyone can understand the lesson's activities.
- Next, do the *Feelings* vocabulary card warm-up (Appendix C) and mix in some vocabulary cards from the previous eight themes.
- Do the alphabet/number card reviews (Appendices D and E) with students.
- Continue reading the chapter book aloud and then ask each student one comprehension question (Appendix Q).
- Do the Video Clip Activity (Appendix H).
- Teach the past-tense *to be* structure for affirmative statements (Appendix L) to the class.
- Play a word wall game of your choice (Appendix K) and sing a few songs (Appendix F) with the class to review concepts previously learned.
- Say goodbye to students individually and have them respond.

Theme Nine: Feelings — Day Three Lesson

Objectives

The student will:

- Practice greeting and saying goodbye
- Practice saying the letters of the alphabet
- Practice saying the numbers 50–60
- Speak about *Feelings* and understand *Feelings* vocabulary
- Use past-tense *to be* verbs to make affirmative and negative statements
- Listen to and understand a chapter book as it is read aloud
- Orally answer comprehension questions about the chapter book
- Analyze and understand language in a short video clip

Materials

- Appendices C/D/E/F/H/K/L/Q, chart paper, vocabulary cards, alphabet cards, number cards, prizes, markers, a read-aloud chapter book, a ball, and a video clip to show with a computer or DVD player

Activities with Informal Evaluations

The description/procedure for each activity below is in its appendix.

- Start the lesson with Circle Time, where the teacher greets each student, the class reads the day's date/activities together in English, and a student translates so everyone can understand the lesson's activities.
- Next, do the *Feelings* vocabulary card warm-up (Appendix C) and mix in some vocabulary cards from the previous eight themes.
- Do the alphabet/number card reviews (Appendices D and E) with students.
- Continue reading the chapter book aloud and then ask each student one comprehension question (Appendix Q).
- Do the Video Clip Activity (Appendix H).
- Review the past-tense *to be* structure for affirmative statements and teach students the past-tense *to be* structure for negative statements (Appendix L).
- Play the word wall game, "Opposites" (Appendix K) and sing a few songs (Appendix F) with the class to review concepts previously learned.
- Say goodbye to students individually and have them respond.

Theme Nine: Feelings — Day Four Lesson

Objectives

The student will:

- Practice greeting and saying goodbye
- Practice saying the letters of the alphabet
- Practice saying the numbers 50–60
- Speak about *Feelings* and understand *Feelings* vocabulary
- Use past-tense *to be* verbs to make statements and questions
- Listen to and understand a chapter book as it is read aloud
- Orally answer comprehension questions about the chapter book
- Analyze and understand language in a short video clip

Materials

- Appendices C/D/E/F/H/K/L/Q, chart paper, vocabulary cards, alphabet cards, number cards, prizes, markers, a read-aloud chapter book, a ball, and a video clip to show with a computer or DVD player

Activities with Informal Evaluations

The description/procedure for each activity below is in its appendix.

- Start the lesson with Circle Time, where the teacher greets each student, the class reads the day's date/activities together in English, and a student translates so everyone can understand the lesson's activities.
- Next, do the *Feelings* vocabulary card warm-up (Appendix C) and mix in some vocabulary cards from the previous eight themes.
- Do the alphabet/number card reviews (Appendices D and E) with students.
- Continue reading the chapter book aloud and then ask each student one comprehension question (Appendix Q).
- Do the Video Clip Activity (Appendix H).
- Review the past-tense *to be* structure for affirmative and negative statements and teach the past-tense *to be* structure for questions (Appendix L).
- Play the "Word" word wall game (Appendix K) to review *was/were* and sing a few songs (Appendix F) with the class to review concepts previously learned.
- Say goodbye to students individually and have them respond.

Theme Nine: Feelings — Day Five Lesson

Objectives

The student will:

- Practice greeting and saying goodbye
- Practice saying the letters of the alphabet
- Speak about *Feelings* and understand *Feelings* vocabulary
- Use past-tense *to be* verbs to create a dialogue
- Listen to and understand a chapter book as it is read aloud
- Orally answer comprehension questions about the chapter book
- Analyze and understand language in a short video clip

Materials

- Appendices C/D/F/H/K/N/Q, chart paper, vocabulary cards, alphabet cards, prizes, markers, a read-aloud chapter book, and a video clip to show with a computer or DVD player

Activities with Informal Evaluations

The description/procedure for each activity below is in its appendix.

- Start the lesson with Circle Time, where the teacher greets each student, the class reads the day's date/activities together in English, and a student translates so everyone can understand the lesson's activities.
- Next, do the *Feelings* vocabulary card warm-up (Appendix C) and mix in some vocabulary cards from the previous eight themes.
- Do the alphabet card review (Appendix D) with students. Because this is the last lesson with a daily alphabet card review, you can spend some extra time on it today and continue working on the number cards next week.
- Continue reading the chapter book aloud and then ask each student one comprehension question (Appendix Q).
- Do the Video Clip Activity (Appendix H) with the class.
- Complete the "Create Your Own Dialogue" activity (Appendix N) with students.
- Play the "Stand and Deliver" word wall game (Appendix K) and sing a few songs (Appendix F) with the class to review concepts previously learned.
- Say goodbye to students individually and have them respond.

Theme Ten: Family — Day One Lesson

Objectives

The student will:

- Practice greeting and saying goodbye
- Practice saying the numbers 50–70
- Speak about *Family* and understand *Family* vocabulary
- Listen to and understand a chapter book as it is read aloud
- Orally answer comprehension questions about the chapter book
- Sing a song about the months of the year
- Review the present-tense verb structure
- Analyze and understand language in a short video clip

Materials

- Appendices C/E/F/H/K/L/Q, chart paper, vocabulary cards, number cards, prizes, markers, a read-aloud chapter book, and a video clip to show with a computer or DVD player

Activities with Informal Evaluations

The description/procedure for each activity below is in its appendix.

- Start the lesson with Circle Time, where the teacher greets each student, the class reads the day's date/activities together in English, and a student translates so everyone can understand the lesson's activities.
- Next, do the *Family* vocabulary card warm-up (Appendix C) and mix in some vocabulary cards from the previous nine themes.
- Do the number card review (Appendix E) with students.
- Continue reading the chapter book aloud and then ask each student one comprehension question (Appendix Q).
- Do the Video Clip Activity (Appendix H) with the class.
- Teach the class "The Month" song (Appendix F) and sing it together.
- Review the present-tense verb structure (Appendix L) with students.
- Play the word wall game, "You Can Act," (Appendix K) to review present-tense concepts.
- Say goodbye to students individually and have them respond.

Theme Ten: Family — Day Two Lesson

Objectives

The student will:

- Practice greeting and saying goodbye
- Practice saying the numbers 50–70
- Speak about *Family* and understand *Family* vocabulary
- Listen to and understand a chapter book as it is read aloud
- Orally answer comprehension questions about the chapter book
- Use the past-tense verb structure in affirmative statements
- Analyze and understand language in a short video clip

Materials

- Appendices C/E/F/H/K/L/Q, chart paper, vocabulary cards, number cards, prizes, markers, a read-aloud chapter book, a ball, and a video clip to show with a computer or DVD player

Activities with Informal Evaluations

The description/procedure for each activity below is in its appendix.

- Start the lesson with Circle Time, where the teacher greets each student, the class reads the day's date/activities together in English, and a student translates so everyone can understand the lesson's activities.
- Next, do the *Family* vocabulary card warm-up (Appendix C) and mix in some vocabulary cards from the previous nine themes.
- Do the number card reviews (Appendix E) with students.
- Read the chapter book aloud and then ask each student one comprehension question (Appendix Q).
- Do the Video Clip Activity (Appendix H) with the class.
- Teach students the past-tense structure for affirmative statements (Appendix L).
- Play a word wall game of your choice (Appendix K) and sing a few songs (Appendix F) with the class to review concepts previously learned.
- Say goodbye to students individually and have them respond.

Theme Ten: Family — Day Three Lesson

Objectives

The student will:

- Practice greeting and saying goodbye
- Practice saying the numbers 50–70
- Speak about *Family* and understand *Family* vocabulary
- Listen to and understand a chapter book as it is read aloud
- Orally answer comprehension questions about the chapter book
- Use the past-tense verbs in affirmative and negative statements
- Analyze and understand language in a short video clip

Materials

- Appendices C/E/F/H/K/L/Q, chart paper, vocabulary cards, number cards, prizes, markers, a read-aloud chapter book, a ball, and a video clip to show with a computer or DVD player

Activities with Informal Evaluations

The description/procedure for each activity below is in its appendix.

- Start the lesson with Circle Time, where the teacher greets each student, the class reads the day's date/activities together in English, and a student translates so everyone can understand the lesson's activities.
- Next, do the *Family* vocabulary card warm-up (Appendix C) and mix in some vocabulary cards from the previous nine themes.
- Do the number card reviews (Appendix E) with students.
- Continue reading the chapter book aloud and then ask each student one comprehension question (Appendix Q).
- Do a Video Clip Activity (Appendix H) with the class.
- Briefly review the past-tense structure for affirmative statements and then teach students the past-tense structure for negative statements (Appendix L).
- Play the word wall game, "Missing in Action," (Appendix K) and sing a few songs (Appendix F) with the class to review concepts previously learned.
- Say goodbye to students individually and have them respond.

Theme Ten: Family — Day Four Lesson

Objectives

The student will:

- Practice greeting and saying goodbye
- Practice saying the numbers 50–70
- Speak about *Family* and understand *Family* vocabulary
- Listen to and understand a chapter book as it is read aloud
- Orally answer comprehension questions about the chapter book
- Use past-tense verbs in statements and questions
- Analyze and understand language in a short video clip

Materials

- Appendices C/E/F/H/K/L/Q, chart paper, vocabulary cards, number cards, prizes, markers, a read-aloud chapter book, a ball, and a video clip to show with a computer or DVD player

Activities with Informal Evaluations

The description/procedure for each activity below is in its appendix.

- Start the lesson with Circle Time, where the teacher greets each student, the class reads the day's date/activities together in English, and a student translates so everyone can understand the lesson's activities.
- Next, do the *Family* vocabulary card warm-up (Appendix C) and mix in some vocabulary cards from the previous nine themes.
- Do the number card reviews (Appendix E) with students.
- Continue reading the chapter book aloud and then ask each student one comprehension question (Appendix Q).
- Do a Video Clip Activity (Appendix H) with the class.
- Briefly review the past-tense structure for affirmative and negative statements and then teach students the past-tense structure for questions (Appendix L).
- Play the word wall game, "Word" (Appendix K) to review past-tense concepts. Sing a few songs (Appendix F) with the class to review other concepts previously learned.
- Say goodbye to students individually and have them respond.

Theme Ten: Family — Day Five Lesson

Objectives

The student will:

- Practice greeting and saying goodbye
- Practice saying the numbers 50–70
- Speak about *Family* and understand *Family* vocabulary
- Listen to and understand a chapter book as it is read aloud
- Orally answer comprehension questions about the chapter book
- Play Musical Chairs to apply knowledge of past-tense verbs
- Analyze and understand language in a short video clip

Materials

- Appendices C/E/F/H/K/Q, chart paper, markers, vocabulary cards, number cards, prizes, a read-aloud chapter book, a music video and a video clip to show with a computer or DVD player

Activities with Informal Evaluations

The description/procedure for each activity below is in its appendix.

- Start the lesson with Circle Time, where the teacher greets each student, the class reads the day's date/activities together in English, and a student translates so everyone can understand the lesson's activities.
- Next, do the *Family* vocabulary card warm-up (Appendix C) and mix in some vocabulary cards from the previous nine themes.
- Do the number card reviews (Appendix E) with students.
- Continue reading the chapter book aloud and then ask each student one comprehension question (Appendix Q).
- Do a Video Clip Activity (Appendix H) with the class.
- Play Musical Chairs with the class to apply their knowledge of past-tense verbs. To do this, set out chairs (one fewer than the number of students playing) and play some music; students must try to sit once the music stops, and whoever is left standing has to create a past-tense sentence or question using the verb and the point of view (first person, etc.) that you tell them.
- Play a word wall game of your choice (Appendix K) and sing a few songs (Appendix F) with the class to review concepts previously learned.
- Say goodbye to students individually and have them respond.

Theme Eleven: Community — Day One Lesson

Objectives

The student will:

- Practice greeting and saying goodbye
- Practice saying the numbers 50–90
- Speak about *Community* and understand *Community* vocabulary
- Listen to and understand a chapter book as it is read aloud
- Orally answer comprehension questions about the chapter book
- Analyze and understand language in a short video clip

Materials

- Appendices C/E/F/H/K/Q, chart paper, vocabulary cards, number cards, prizes, markers, a read-aloud chapter book, and a video clip to show with a computer or DVD player

Activities with Informal Evaluations

The description/procedure for each activity below is in its appendix.

- Start the lesson with Circle Time, where the teacher greets each student, the class reads the day's date/activities together in English, and a student translates so everyone can understand the lesson's activities.
- Next, do the *Community* vocabulary card warm-up (Appendix C) and mix in some vocabulary cards from the previous ten themes.
- Do the number card reviews (Appendix E) with students.
- Continue reading the chapter book aloud and then ask each student one comprehension question (Appendix Q).
- Do a Video Clip Activity (Appendix H) with the class.
- Do the "Guess It!" Activity (Appendix H) with students.
- Play the word wall game, "It's a New Word," (Appendix K) and sing a few songs (Appendix F) with the class to review concepts previously learned.
- Say goodbye to students individually and have them respond.

Theme Eleven: Community — Day Two Lesson

Objectives

The student will:

- Practice greeting and saying goodbye
- Practice saying the numbers 50–90
- Speak about *Community* and understand *Community* vocabulary
- Apply knowledge of articles in a game
- Listen to and understand a chapter book as it is read aloud
- Orally answer comprehension questions about the chapter book
- Analyze and understand language in a short video clip

Materials

- Appendices C/E/F/H/I/L/Q, chart paper, vocabulary cards, number cards, prizes, markers, a read-aloud chapter book, a ball, and a video clip to show with a computer or DVD player

Activities with Informal Evaluations

The description/procedure for each activity below is in its appendix.

- Start the lesson with Circle Time, where the teacher greets each student, the class reads the day's date/activities together in English, and a student translates so everyone can understand the lesson's activities.
- Next, do the *Community* vocabulary card warm-up (Appendix C) and mix in some vocabulary cards from the previous ten themes.
- Do the number card reviews (Appendix E) with students.
- Continue reading the chapter book aloud and then ask each student one comprehension question (Appendix Q).
- Do a Video Clip Activity (Appendix H) with the class.
- Review the articles structure (Appendix L) and then play a game of "Simon Says" (Appendix I) where students can only follow your directions when you use: "a" in the commands for the first game, "an" in the commands for the second game, and "the" in the commands for the third game.
- Sing a few songs (Appendix F) with the class to review concepts previously learned.
- Say goodbye to students individually and have them respond.

Theme Eleven: Community — Day Three Lesson

Objectives

The student will:

- Practice greeting and saying goodbye
- Practice saying the numbers 50–90
- Speak about *Community* and understand *Community* vocabulary
- Listen to and understand a chapter book as it is read aloud
- Orally answer comprehension questions about the chapter book
- Use the articles *a* and *an* in sentences
- Use *there*, articles, and past-tense/present-tense verbs in an unscramble activity
- Analyze and understand language in a short video clip

Materials

- Appendices C/E/F/H/K/L/Q, chart paper, vocabulary cards, number cards, prizes, markers, a read-aloud chapter book, and a video clip to show with a computer or DVD player

Activities with Informal Evaluations

The description/procedure for each activity below is in its appendix.

- Start the lesson with Circle Time, where the teacher greets each student, the class reads the day's date/activities together in English, and a student translates so everyone can understand the lesson's activities.
- Next, do the *Community* vocabulary card warm-up (Appendix C) and mix in some vocabulary cards from the previous ten themes.
- Do the number card reviews (Appendix E) with students.
- Continue reading the chapter book aloud and then ask each student one comprehension question (Appendix Q).
- Do a Video Clip Activity (Appendix H) with the class.
- Review the articles structure for *a* and *an* (Appendix L) with the class.
- Do the "Funky Phrases" activity (Appendix H) with students.
- If time, play the word wall game, "Mystery Word," (Appendix K) to apply knowledge of the *a* and *an* articles.
- Say goodbye to students individually and have them respond.

Theme Eleven: Community — Day Four Lesson

Objectives

The student will:

- Practice greeting and saying goodbye
- Practice saying the numbers 50–90
- Speak about *Community* and understand *Community* vocabulary
- Listen to a chapter book as it is read aloud and orally answer comprehension questions
- Apply knowledge of the *there* structure in a presentation activity
- Analyze and understand language in a short video clip
- Ask questions and give answers using the past-tense structure

Materials

- Appendices C/E/F/H/K/L/Q, chart paper, vocabulary cards, number cards, prizes, markers, a read-aloud chapter book, a ball, and a video clip to show with a computer or DVD player

Activities with Informal Evaluations

The description/procedure for each activity below is in its appendix.

- Start the lesson with Circle Time, where the teacher greets each student, the class reads the day's date/activities together in English, and a student translates so everyone can understand the lesson's activities.
- Next, do the *Community* vocabulary card warm-up (Appendix C) and mix in some vocabulary cards from the previous ten themes.
- Do the number card reviews (Appendix E) with students.
- Continue reading the chapter book aloud and then ask each student one comprehension question (Appendix Q).
- Do a Video Clip Activity (Appendix H) with the class.
- Review the *there* structure (Appendix L) with the class. Then have students do and present an activity where they have to look around the school building/grounds to answer questions related to school objects (Example- How many chairs are in room 106? How many bathrooms are in the east wing?) Then students must present their findings to the class using the proper *there* structure (Example- There are 10 chairs in room 106. There was one bathroom in the east wing.)
- Play the word wall game, "Observation," (Appendix K) and sing a few songs (Appendix F) with the class to review concepts previously learned.
- Say goodbye to students individually and have them respond.

Theme Eleven: Community — Day Five Lesson

Objectives

The student will:

- Practice greeting and saying goodbye
- Practice saying the numbers 50–90
- Speak about *Community* and understand *Community* vocabulary
- Listen to and understand a chapter book as it is read aloud
- Orally answer comprehension questions about the chapter book
- Analyze and understand language in a short video clip
- Ask questions and give answers using the past-tense structure
- Use future verbs in affirmative sentences

Materials

- Appendices C/E/F/H/K/L/Q, chart paper, vocabulary cards, number cards, prizes, markers, a read-aloud chapter book, a ball, and a video clip to show with a computer or DVD player

Activities with Informal Evaluations

The description/procedure for each activity below is in its appendix.

- Start the lesson with Circle Time, where the teacher greets each student, the class reads the day's date/activities together in English, and a student translates so everyone can understand the lesson's activities.
- Next, do the *Community* vocabulary card warm-up (Appendix C) and mix in some vocabulary cards from the previous ten themes.
- Do the number card reviews (Appendix E) with students.
- Continue reading the chapter book aloud and then ask each student one comprehension question (Appendix Q).
- Do a Video Clip Activity (Appendix H) with the class.
- Teach students the future verb structure for affirmative statements (Appendix L).
- Do the "Student Questionnaire" activity (Appendix H) with the class.
- If time, play a word wall game of your choice (Appendix K) and sing a few songs (Appendix F) with the class to review concepts previously learned.
- Say goodbye to students individually and have them respond.

Theme Twelve: Activities — Day One Lesson

Objectives

The student will:

- Practice greeting and saying goodbye
- Practice saying the numbers 50–100
- Speak about *Activities* and understand *Activities* vocabulary
- Listen to and understand a chapter book as it is read aloud
- Orally answer comprehension questions about the chapter book
- Use future verbs in affirmative and negative statements
- Review prepositions *on/in* and sing a song about these prepositions
- Analyze and understand language in a short video clip

Materials

- Appendices C/E/F/H/K/L/Q, chart paper, vocabulary cards, number cards, prizes, markers, a read-aloud chapter book, a ball, a box, a stuffed animal (dog), and a video clip to show with a computer or DVD player

Activities with Informal Evaluations

The description/procedure for each activity below is in its appendix.

- Start the lesson with Circle Time, where the teacher greets each student, the class reads the day's date/activities together in English, and a student translates so everyone can understand the lesson's activities.
- Next, do the *Activities* vocabulary card warm-up (Appendix C) and mix in some vocabulary cards from the previous eleven themes.
- Do the number card reviews (Appendix E) with students.
- Continue reading the chapter book aloud and then ask each student one comprehension question (Appendix Q).
- Do a Video Clip Activity (Appendix H) with the class.
- Review the future verb structure for affirmative statements and teach students the future verb structure for negative statements (Appendix L).
- Introduce students to the "Where Is the Dog?" song (Appendix F); teach/sing the first verse only to review the prepositions *in/on.*
- Play the word wall game, "Line Up," (Appendix K) to review previous concepts.
- Say goodbye to students individually and have them respond.

Theme Twelve: Activities — Day Two Lesson

Objectives

The student will:

- Practice greeting and saying goodbye
- Practice saying the numbers 50–100
- Speak about *Activities* and understand *Activities* vocabulary
- Apply prepositions *near/far from/before/after/below/above/beside* to a song, an activity, and word wall words
- Listen to a chapter book as it is read aloud and orally answer comprehension questions
- Analyze and understand language in a short video clip

Materials

- Appendices C/E/F/H/K/Q, chart paper, vocabulary cards, number cards, prizes, markers, a read-aloud chapter book, a box, a stuffed animal (dog), and a video clip to show with a computer or DVD player

Activities with Informal Evaluations

The description/procedure for each activity below is in its appendix.

- Start the lesson with Circle Time, where the teacher greets each student, the class reads the day's date/activities together in English, and a student translates so everyone can understand the lesson's activities.
- Next, do the *Activities* vocabulary card warm-up (Appendix C) and mix in some vocabulary cards from the previous eleven themes.
- Do the number card reviews (Appendix E) with students.
- Read the chapter book aloud and then ask each student one comprehension question (Appendix Q).
- Do a Video Clip Activity (Appendix H) with the class.
- Teach the prepositions of location *near/far from/before/after/below/above/beside*; the explanation for teaching these propositions is with the Kinesthetic Practice Activity (Appendix H). Next, do the Kinesthetic Practice Activity (Appendix H) to practice all these prepositions with students.
- Teach/sing the rest of the "Where Is the Dog?" song (Appendix F) to practice all song prepositions with students.
- Play the word wall game, "Locate It," (Appendix K) to review previous concepts.
- Say goodbye to students individually and have them respond.

Theme Twelve: Activities — Day Three Lesson

Objectives

The student will:

- Practice greeting and saying goodbye
- Practice saying the numbers 50–100
- Speak about *Activities* and understand *Activities* vocabulary
- Use various verb-tense structures to create a dialogue
- Listen to and understand a chapter book as it is read aloud
- Orally answer comprehension questions about the chapter book
- Sing a song about the common prepositions

Materials

- Appendices C/E/H/K/N/Q, chart paper, vocabulary cards, number cards, prizes, markers, a read-aloud chapter book, and a video clip to show with a computer or DVD player

Activities with Informal Evaluations

The description/procedure for each activity below is in its appendix.

- Start the lesson with Circle Time, where the teacher greets each student, the class reads the day's date/activities together in English, and a student translates so everyone can understand the lesson's activities.
- Next, do the *Activities* vocabulary card warm-up (Appendix C) and mix in some vocabulary cards from the previous eleven themes.
- Do the number card reviews (Appendix E) with students.
- Continue reading the chapter book aloud and then ask each student one comprehension question (Appendix Q).
- Do a Video Clip Activity (Appendix H) with the class.
- Do the "Create Your Own Dialogue" activity (Appendix N) with the class.
- Play the word wall game, "Stand and Deliver" (Appendix K) to review previous concepts.
- Say goodbye to students individually and have them respond.

Theme Twelve: Activities — Day Four Lesson

Objectives

The student will:

- Practice greeting and saying goodbye
- Practice saying the numbers 1–100
- Speak about *Activities* and understand *Activities* vocabulary
- Use future-tense verbs in statements and questions
- Listen to and understand a chapter book as it is read aloud
- Orally answer comprehension questions about the chapter book
- Analyze and understand language in a short video clip

Materials

- Appendices C/E/F/H/K/L/Q, chart paper, vocabulary cards, number cards, prizes, markers, a read-aloud chapter book, a ball, and a video clip to show with a computer or DVD player

Activities with Informal Evaluations

The description/procedure for each activity below is in its appendix.

- Start the lesson with Circle Time, where the teacher greets each student, the class reads the day's date/activities together in English, and a student translates so everyone can understand the lesson's activities.
- Next, do the *Activities* vocabulary card warm-up (Appendix C) and mix in some vocabulary cards from the previous eleven themes.
- Do the number card reviews (Appendix E) with students.
- Continue reading the chapter book aloud and then ask each student one comprehension question (Appendix Q).
- Do a Video Clip Activity (Appendix H) with the class.
- Review the future verbs structure for affirmative and negative statements and teach students the future verbs structure for questions (Appendix L).
- Play the word wall game "It's Your Future" (Appendix K) and sing a few songs (Appendix F) with the class to review concepts previously learned.
- Say goodbye to students individually and have them respond.

Theme Twelve: Activities — Day Five Lesson

Objectives

The student will:

- Practice greeting and saying goodbye
- Practice saying the numbers 1–100
- Speak about *Activities* and understand *Activities* vocabulary
- Finish the chapter book and share their favorite part
- Analyze and understand language in a short video clip
- Apply knowledge of future-tense verbs in a presentation of their future plans

Materials

- Appendices C/E/F/H/K/L/Q, chart paper, vocabulary cards, number cards, prizes, markers, a read-aloud chapter book, a ball, and a video clip to show with a computer or DVD player

Activities with Informal Evaluations

The description/procedure for each activity below is in its appendix.

- Start this final lesson with Circle Time, where the teacher greets each student, the class reads the day's date/activities together in English, and a student translates so everyone can understand the lesson's activities.
- Next, do the *Activities* vocabulary card warm-up (Appendix C) and mix in some vocabulary cards from the previous eleven themes.
- Do the number card reviews (Appendix E) with students.
- Finish reading the chapter book aloud and then ask each student to share his or her favorite part of the story (Appendix Q).
- Do a Video Clip Activity (Appendix H) with the class.
- Briefly review the future verbs structure (Appendix L) and have students create some future-tense sentences about what they will do after English class ends. Have students present their future plans to the class.
- If there is time, play a word wall game of your choice (Appendix K) and sing a few songs (Appendix F) with the class to review concepts previously learned.
- Say goodbye to students individually and have them respond.

If you are continuing on with *ESL in the Middle: Lessons Guide for Teaching Intermediate English*, you can find it and other products at www.bilinguallearner.com.

Appendix A: Parent Notification Letter

August 2014

Dear Parent,

Your child, ______________________________________, has been selected to work 5 days a week in a small group to improve her/his English speaking and understanding. While your child is making progress in communicating in the English language, we would like to take this opportunity to give him/her some extra English language support. These classes will meet Monday through Friday for 2 hours in Ms./Mr. ______________________'s classroom. It is very important that your child attend each class. If you have any questions, please call me at school. Thank you very much for your support.

Sincerely,

____

Teacher

SPANISH VERSION

Agosto 2014

Querido Padre,

Su niño/a, ____________________________________, ha sido seleccionado para trabajar 5 días a la semana en un pequeño grupo para mejorar su Inglés oral y comprensión. Mientras su niño/a esta progresando de una manera consistente en la comunicación del inglés, nos gustaría darle esta oportunidad a su niño/a con un apoyo extra en inglés. Estas clases serán de lunes hasta viernes por 2 horas en el salón de la señora/del señor _________________________. Es muy importante que su niño/a atienda a cada clase. Muchas gracias por su apoyo. Si tiene preguntas, por favor llámeme a la escuela.

Sinceramente,

____

Maestra/o

Appendix B: ESL Diagnostic Test

Name: ______________________________ **Birthday:** ____________
Primary Language: __________________ **Date:** ___________
Grade: _________
Student's ESL Level and number of correct tallies at this level (TO BE ASSIGNED AFTER ASSESSMENT): _____/_____

Directions: Complete the following assessment with each student in your group right before you start the Theme One lessons. Administer this assessment to students individually by sitting in a quiet place with them and asking them each question/prompt below in English. You will need to use the picture below and a box of 12 crayons for some of the questions/prompts. Write down the student's answer, and move to the next question/prompt. After the student has finished a level of the assessment, have him/her do a quiet activity near you while you score the level by making a tally in the correct/incorrect column using the attached Scoring Key. After you've made all the tallies, count them and reference the attached Scoring Guide for that level to determine whether you should administer the next level of the assessment. Also, use the Scoring Guide for each level to determine the student's ESL level, and write it on the correct line above. On that same line, also write down the number of correct tallies the student achieved at that level because that number will help you identify the student's level of proficiency at each level. Give this same assessment again after the Theme Four lessons to see what progress the student has made and to determine further areas of focus for the student. When reassessing, it is best to start with a blank copy of the assessment and begin again at the assessment level that the student achieved the last time he/she was evaluated.

Beginning English Speaking (BES) Level Scoring Guide

Direct the student to respond to all of the following questions/prompts by answering you in English after you read him/her the prompt in English. If the student scores three or more errors, there is no need to continue with the assessment because he/she is at the Beginning English Speaking (BES) Level. Make sure to mark "BES Level" on the front page and also include the number of correct tallies to show his/her proficiency at this level. Alternatively, if the student scores two errors or fewer, continue onto the Intermediate Level of the assessment.

	CORRECT	INCORRECT
1. What is your name? ____________________	______	______
2. Where are you from? ____________________	______	______
3. Tell me how you spell your name. ____________	______	______
4. How old are you? ____________________	______	______
(Put a 12-count box of crayons on the desk for the next three questions/prompts.)		
5. How many crayons are in the box? ____________	______	______
6. Put a crayon on your paper. ______________	______	______
7. Draw a road with the crayon. ______________	______	______
(Show the picture on page B-1 for the next five questions.)		
8. ***(Point to the woman.)*** **What is this?** ____________	______	______
9. ***(Point to the bird.)*** **What is this? Tell me what this is in a sentence.**		
____________________________________	______	______
10. This is a tree. There are five ______________.	______	______
11. ***(Point to the people.)*** **In this picture, what are they doing?**		
Tell me in a sentence. ____________________	______	______
12. In this picture, the dog is resting. He was playing all day before this picture was taken. Now he just wants to rest. Does he feel angry or tired now?		
____________________________________	______	______

End of Level. Score answers to determine whether student should proceed to next level.

Intermediate English Speaking (IES) Level Scoring Guide

Direct the student to respond to all of the following questions/prompts by answering you in English after you read him/her the prompt in English. If the student scores three or more errors, he/she stays at the Intermediate English Speaking (IES) Level. Make sure to mark "IES Level" on the front page and also include the correct number of tallies to show his/her proficiency at this level. Alternatively, if the student scores two errors or fewer, continue onto the Advanced Level of the assessment.

CORRECT **INCORRECT**

(Show the picture on page B-1 again for the next three questions.)

1. **What is at the bottom of the picture?** __________________ ______ ______

2. **There are two people in this picture. How many fingers and toes do they have, total?** ***(Have students draw a picture of each hand and foot and then count up the fingers and toes if they can't do the mental math in their head or if this question is confusing to them.)***

   _____ ______ ______

3. **What do you think the man and woman in the picture did yesterday? Tell me in a sentence.**

   ____ ______ ______

4. **What fruit or vegetable did you eat yesterday? Tell me in a sentence.**

   ____ ______ ______

5. **What fruit or vegetable will you eat next week? Tell me in a sentence.**

   ____ ______ ______

6. **When is your birthday?** __________________________ ______ ______

7. **Tell me some good things about your family in a sentence.**

   ____ ______ ______

(For the next two prompts, ask student to repeat the following sentences after you; say each only once.)

8. **I like to eat bananas.** ____________________________ ______ ______

9. **The girl played soccer, and the boy played tennis.**

   ____ ______ ______

End of Level. Score answers to determine whether student should proceed to next level.

Advanced English Speaking (AES) Level Scoring Guide

Direct the student to respond to all of the following questions/prompts by answering you in English after you read him/her the prompt in English. After completing this assessment with the student, mark "AES Level" on the front page. Also include the number of correct tallies on the front page because that number will show the student's level of proficiency within the AES Level.

	CORRECT	INCORRECT
(Show the picture on page B-1 again for the next four questions below.)		
1. Tell me three things you think could happen in this picture.		
______________________________	______	______
______________________________	______	______
______________________________	______	______
2. Now, you ask me something. Ask me a question about the people in this picture.		
______________________________	______	______
3. *(Point to the forest setting.)* Where are the man and the woman? Tell me in a sentence.		
______________________________	______	______
4. *(Point to the forest setting.)* This is where I went last year. Tell me in a sentence where I went last year. ______________________	______	______
5. Tell me how to get to the bathroom from where we are now.		
______________________________		
______________________________	______	______
I'm going to tell you some words from the picture. You tell me if they are the same or different. Do these words from the picture sound the same?		
6. Boot/bench: Are they the same or different? ________	______	______
7. Girl/curl: Are they the same or different? __________	______	______
8. Grass/grass: Are they the same or different? _________	______	______

End of Assessment

Scoring Key

Beginning English Speaker (BES)
Intermediate English Speaker (IES)
Advanced English Speaker (AES)

Beginning Level

1. student's name
2. student correctly says where he/she is from
3. student correctly spells his/her first name correctly
4. student's age
5. 12
6. student obeys command correctly
7. student draws a road
8. a woman (or any correct female or non-gender human noun)
9. This/It is a bird.
10. trees
11. They are sitting (or talking, resting).
12. tired

Intermediate Level

1. grass, bird, dog, or animal(s)
2. 40
3. student uses sentence with past-tense verb or past-continuous verb to correctly state what the man and the woman did yesterday
4. student uses sentence to correctly name a fruit or vegetable that they ate yesterday
5. I will eat a/an *(name of a fruit or vegetable)* next week.
6. student's birthday
7. student uses sentence to correctly state two or more good things about their family
8. student correctly pronounces sentence
9. student correctly pronounces sentence

Advanced Level

1. student uses modal/future verbs and main verbs to make predictions about the picture
2. student asks you a correctly worded question about the picture
3. student correctly uses sentence to state the location of the man and the woman
4. student correctly uses past tense to state that you (teacher) went to a forest/park location last year
5. student gives correct directions to bathroom
6. different
7. different
8. same

Appendix C: Vocabulary Cards

Topics: Home, School, Nature, Personal Hygiene, The Body, Occupations, Technology, Transportation, Feelings, Family, Community, and Activities

These vocabulary cards are easy to make and a great warm-up activity to teach new words or review old ones. To make the cards, get a stack of index cards and write each word on a separate card in bold, clear printing. Under the word, draw or paste a small picture of the object. There are many free clipart websites where you can find pictures of all of these vocabulary words. You can type "free clipart" into an internet search engine and pick from any of the website choices there. Some of my favorite clipart websites are: classroomclipart.com, clker.com, and pdclipart.com.

After you have made your vocabulary cards, spend 5–10 minutes each day showing students the cards and having them name the object. I like to work in a round-robin style, allowing students to try multiple cards and letting them hold any card they name correctly. At the end of the warm-up, I usually let the student with the most cards pick a small prize. For adults, chocolate or a canned juice/soda is usually a welcomed reward! I also tell students that if I see they are quietly paying attention to others trying to pronounce their cards, I will award them an extra turn. Below are the words/pictures to put on each card, organized by topic.

School: desk, pen, pencil, crayons, stapler, paper, clock, scissors, tape, glue, book, map, trash can, bathroom, markers, computer, bookshelf, cabinet, classroom, bus, box, letter, number

Home: table, chair, sofa, lamp, door, window, house, floor, bathtub, toilet, roof, bed, closet, refrigerator, stove, radio, television, stairs, wall, sink

Nature: dog, cat, tree, girl, boy, baby, man, woman, horse, cow, bird, plant, fish, pig, spider, bee, duck, flower, grass, sun, moon, cloud, star, sky

Personal Hygiene: brush, comb, soap, toothbrush, toothpaste, towel, tissue, toilet paper, glasses, razor, shower, bath, clothes, shoes, pants, shirt, socks, coat, shampoo

The Body: finger, toe, tooth, knee, shoulder, neck, head, hair, leg, hand, foot, face, lip, ear, eye, mouth, nose, heart, brain, stomach, chest, bone, muscle, back, tongue

Occupations: teacher, doctor, police officer, fireman, janitor, librarian, astronaut, veterinarian, pilot, truck driver, painter, singer, chef, farmer, soldier, construction worker, bus driver, maid, gardener, secretary, cashier, lawyer

Technology: computer, keyboard, printer, thermometer, watch, video camera, telephone, fax, microwave, DVD player, camera, photocopier, telescope, space shuttle, iPod, stereo, calculator

Transportation: car, van, bus, motorcycle, bike, train, skateboard, airplane, boat, ship, sled, truck, taxi, helicopter, tractor

Feelings: happy, sad, angry (mad), tired, excited, frustrated, sick, bored, miserable, loving, scared, anxious, hurt, strange, calm, confused, embarrassed, homesick, hungry, thirsty

Family Members: husband, wife, daughter, son, mother, father, sister, brother, grandma, grandpa, grandson, granddaughter, aunt, uncle, cousin, stepsister, stepbrother, stepmother, stepfather, niece, nephew

Community: airport, bus station, train station, mall, farm, subway, factory, ranch, museum, harbor, skyscraper, road, gas station, post office, bank, office, church, courthouse, cinema, park, police station, grocery store, library

Activities: dancing, exercising, shopping, cooking, playing sports, sleeping, eating, reading, talking, working, resting, writing, watching television, watching movies, playing music, studying, sitting, walking, standing in line

Here Stephanie teaches a lesson with vocabulary cards.

Appendix D: Alphabet Cards

These cards are notebook paper-sized and laminated with all the letters of the alphabet on one side. Each student gets a card once or twice per week during Circle Time and practices pronouncing each square of the card using the following steps:

- Using a card, teacher points to the letter to say. Students put their finger on the correct letter on their own card.
- Teacher says the letter/sound while students listen. Then students repeat as a group.
- Individual students repeat the letter/sound (round-robin style is fine).
- The above steps are repeated with the next letter.

We do this once or twice a week at the beginning of the lesson for 5–10 minutes, saying all the letters/sounds of the alphabet. After students practice this activity for a week or so, try letting a student point out the letter on the card and make sure the other students put their finger on the correct letter and pronounce it correctly. The student leader can ask others to re-pronounce, if necessary.

Alphabet Cards

Aa	Bb	Cc	Dd	Ee
Ff	Gg	Hh	Ii	Jj
Kk	Ll	Mm	Nn	Oo
Pp	Qq	Rr	Ss	Tt
Uu	Vv	Ww	Xx	Yy/Zz

Appendix E: Number Cards

These cards are also notebook paper-sized and laminated with numbers 1–50 on one side and numbers 51–100 on the other side. Each student gets a card each day during Circle Time and practices pronouncing each square of the card using the following steps:

- Using a card, teacher points to the number to say. Students put their finger on the correct number on their own card.
- Teacher says the number while students listen. Then students repeat as a group.
- Individual students repeat the number (round-robin style is fine).
- The above steps are repeated with the next number.

We do this each day at the beginning of the lesson for 10 minutes. First, as a group, we count off each number that we have already been practicing, and then we slow down to spend more time using the first three steps above steps on the newest set of 10 numbers that we are learning. After students practice this activity for a week or so, try letting a student point out the number on the card and make sure the other students put their finger on the correct number and pronounce it correctly. The student leader can ask others to re-pronounce, if necessary.

The classroom is set up for a number card activity.

Number Card

Front:

1	2	3	4	5
6	7	8	9	10
11	12	13	14	15
16	17	18	19	20
21	22	23	24	25
26	27	28	29	30
31	32	33	34	35
36	37	38	39	40
41	42	43	44	45
46	47	48	49	50

Back:

51	52	53	54	55
56	57	58	59	60
61	62	63	64	65
66	67	68	69	70
71	72	73	74	75
76	77	78	79	80
81	82	83	84	85
86	87	88	89	90
91	92	93	94	95
96	97	98	99	100

Appendix F: Songs and Chants

Songs and chants are an engaging and active way for students to practice the language concepts they have learned with no pressure. All of these can be sung by anyone, no matter how untrained the singer. Here are some guidelines for teaching songs:

- Put all songs on chart paper.
- Go over key vocabulary in the songs (for strategies, see Appendix R).
- Students should follow along as the teacher points to the words, pronouncing each word (for readers and non-readers alike).
- Discuss the meaning of the song and even have a student orally translate it into the native language, if necessary.
- Sing the song/chant with the class.
- After students have learned a song, sing it with them every few days to practice, have fun, and review the concept during the warm-up or closing parts of the lesson.

Also, after students get to know the song, try having one student point out the lyrics on chart paper and another student perform any song hand motions, while the rest of the class follows along.

Tuning the guitars for songs and chants.

"To Be" Chant/Hand Clap

**This chant is best sung to the beat of clapped hands/thighs in a rapid 1-2 rhythm.*

I am, *(one hand clap)*
You are, *(one hand clap)*
He is, she is, it is. *(three faster thigh claps—one for each conjugation)*
We are, *(one hand clap)*
They are, *(one hand clap)*
Present-Tense To Be! *(three faster thigh claps—one for each word)*

Past-Tense "To Be" Chant

**This chant is best sung to the beat of clapped hands/thighs in a rapid 1-2 rhythm.*

I was, *(one hand clap)*
You were, *(one hand clap)*
He was, she was, it was. *(three faster thigh claps—one for each conjugation)*
We were, *(one hand clap)*
They were, *(one hand clap)*
Past-Tense To Be! *(three faster thigh claps—one for each word)*

Present-Tense Chant

**This chant is best sung to the beat of clapped hands/thighs in a rapid 1-2 rhythm.*

I chant, *(one hand clap)*
You chant, *(one hand clap)*
He chants, she chants, it chants. *(three faster thigh claps—one for each conjugation)*
We chant, *(one hand clap)*
They chant, *(one hand clap)*
Present-Tense Verbs! *(three faster thigh claps—one for each word)*

"This and That" Chant

**This chant has a flowing 1-2-3-4 rhythm.*

These are the flowers
That house those bees
And that is the bird
That lives in this tree.

"Alphabet Song"

**It's lovely to play guitar along with this song; the chords are simple and listed below in bold caps. You can type the capital letters below into a search engine with the phrase "guitar chords" and you'll find the correct chord fingering if you don't know chords and would like to learn.*

D G D
A, b, c, d, e, f, g,

G D A D
H, i, j, k, l, m, n, o, p

D G
Q, r, s,

D A
T, u, v,

D G D A
W, x, y, and z,

D G D
Now I know my a-b-c's

G D A D
Next time won't you sing with me!

"This Is the Way" Song

**This song is sung to the tune of "Here We Go Round the Mulberry Bush" and is fun and easy to accompany with the guitar (repeating chords G, D7). You can type the above song title into a search engine with the phrase "guitar chords" and you'll find the correct chord fingering if you don't know chords. Students can do accompanying hand movements to show showering, brushing teeth, and combing hair while they sing.*

G
This is the way we take a shower,

D7
Take a shower,

D7
Take a shower,

G **D7** **G**
This is the way we take a shower when we wake up in the morning.

G
This is the way we brush our teeth,

D7
Brush our teeth,

D7
Brush our teeth,

G **D7** **G**
This is the way we brush our teeth when we wake up in the morning.

G
This is the way we comb our hair,

D7
Comb our hair,

D7
Comb our hair,

G **D7** **G**
This is the way we comb our hair when we wake up in the morning.

"Have You Seen the Ghost of John?" Song

**It's lovely to play guitar along with this song; the chords are simple and listed below in bold caps. You can type the capital letters below into a search engine with the phrase "guitar chords" and you'll find the correct chord fingering if you don't know chords and would like to learn. If you don't know the melody of this song, you can search it in Google or YouTube to listen to it.*

Am
Have you seen the ghost of John?

C **Am**
Long white bones and the rest all gooooooooone,

E7
Oooooooooooooooooooooooooh!

Am **Em Am**
Wouldn't it be chilly with no skin on!

Days of the Week Song

**This song is song to the tune of "Row, Row, Row Your Boat." Additionally, you can accompany this song with the guitar; the chords are simple and listed below in bold caps. In fact, if you don't know how to play guitar but want to learn, this is a perfect song to start with because the chords are very easy and there are only two of them. Also, if you don't know chords, you can type the capital letters below into a search engine with the phrase "guitar chords" and you'll find the correct chord fingering.*

A
Days, days, days of the week,
First Sunday, then Monday,
Tuesday, Wednesday, Thursday, Friday,

E **A**
And then there's Saturday!

The Month Song

**This song is sung to the tune of "Clementine" and is fun and easy to accompany with the guitar. The chords are simple and listed below in bold caps. You can type "Clementine" into a search engine with the phrase "guitar chords" you'll find the correct chord fingering if you don't know chords.*

G
There are twelve months,

G
There are twelve months,

G D7
There are twelve months in this tune,

D7 G
January, February,

D7 G
March and April, May and June.

G
Then there's July,

G
And there's August,

G D7
September, October, too,

D7 G
Don't forget about November

D7 G
And December ends the group!

"Where Is the Dog?" Song

**C G7 C*This song is sung to the tune of "Three Blind Mice" and is fun and easy to accompany with the guitar. The chords are simple and listed below in bold caps. You can type "Three Blind Mice" into a search engine with the phrase "guitar chords" and you'll find the correct chord fingering if you don't know chords. Before starting this song, it is good to review the* on/in *prepositions by writing them on chart paper and showing students their meanings again. Tell them the song will also introduce them to some new prepositions:* near/far from *and* above/below. *To use visuals and TPR for this activity, get a box and a dog stuffed toy and act out the song with these two objects as you sing it with students. Then, once students know the song, give them (or have them make/draw using paper and cardboard) their own small box and dog toy and they can act out the song along with you. Once students get familiar with the entire song, you can have them change the prepositions in the song to act out the song with the dog in different locations relative to the box.*

C G7 C
Where is the dog?

C G7 C
Where is the dog?

C G C G C
Is he in the box? Is he on the box?

C
Is he in the box? No, he's not!
C
Is he on the box? Yes, he is!

C G7 C G7 C
He is on the box, he is on the box!

C G7 C
Where is the dog?

C G7 C
Where is the dog?

C G C G C
Is he near the box? Is he far from the box?

C
Is he near the box? No, he's not!

C
Is he far from the box? Yes, he is!

C G7 C G7 C
He is far from the box, he is far from the box!

C G7 C
Where is the dog?

C G7 C
Where is the dog?

C G C G C
Is he below the box? Is he above the box?

C
Is he below the box? No, he's not!

C
Is he above the box? Yes, he is!

C G7 C G7 C
He is above the box, he is above the box!

Stephanie sings "Where is the Dog?" with first graders.

Appendix G: Short Stories

These little stories are a simple way to tie together all the concepts the students have been taught during the week's ESL lessons. First, discuss, define, or review any necessary vocabulary, verb conjugations, and/or grammar structures in the story. Write the story on chart paper and read it slowly to students, pantomiming all the parts of the story to help them understand. Then read it again, pointing out each word as you read while students only listen. Read it a third time, inviting students to read along (even young children who can't read will eagerly try to "read" along with you, saying many incorrect words or babbling; this is fine). Finally, have a student translate the story so everyone can understand its meaning. Then have students answer the questions orally.

Story #1: "Friends at School"

Two friends at school are named Mary and Joe. They are both students. Mary is a girl. Joe is a boy. They ride the bus. They are both good students. I am the teacher of Mary and Joe.

1. Who is Mary?
2. Are Joe and Mary friends?
3. Where are Joe and Mary?
4. Who is the boy?
5. Who is the teacher?

Story #2: "Friends at Home"

Mary and Joe ride the bus home. Can Mary do homework at Joe's house? Joe says yes. Can Joe use Mary's spelling book? Mary says that the spelling book is on the chair. She gets the book for Joe. They do spelling homework at the table. Mary spells her name with the letters M-A-R-Y, and Joe spells his name with the letters J-O-E.

1. Joe and Mary ride the _______.
2. Can Joe use the book?
3. Where is the book?
4. Spell Mary's name.
5. Spell Joe's name.

Story #3: "Friends in the Garden"

Mary and Joe play in the garden. This is fun. Joe sees a bee in a tree. Mary sees that bee. Joe and Mary see a spider in a flower. This is a pretty flower. There are 10 trees in the yard and 20 bees in the trees.

1. Where do Joe and Mary play?
2. What do they see in the yard?
3. How many bees are in the trees?
4. Do Joe and Mary have fun?

Story #4: "Clean Friends"

Mary and Joe like to look good at school. Mary combs her hair before school. Joe brushes his teeth after breakfast. Today is Mary's birthday. Joe gives her a new comb. Joe says "Happy Birthday" to Mary. Mary is happy.

5. Who has a birthday today?
6. Who says "Happy Birthday"?
7. What does Joe give Mary?
8. Is Mary happy or mad?

Being an English Language Learner herself many years ago, Molin (right) gave Stephanie many tips for teaching English in Mozambique. The little nugget in the middle is Keanu, Molin's son.

Appendix H: Activities

Circle Speaking Activity

This is an oral repetition activity that works well after the main part of the lesson has taken place. It's good to use some of the structures and vocabulary from the lesson in this activity. Be sure to define/explain any new vocabulary or concepts. Write one of the prompts below on the chalk/whiteboard with the corresponding choices/word bank for the blank part. Read the prompt and corresponding word bank aloud so all students can hear the correct pronunciation. Read them aloud again, and have students repeat after you. Then have each student say the sentence with his/her own answer for the blank.

**I've included one example of a prompt for each week; for the other days, you can create prompts based on your lessons.*

**You might shorten the prompts to one sentence for young children who can't read yet.*

Week 1 Prompt

This is a ________________. There are five ________________________.

WORD BANK: desk/s, pen/s, pencil/s, crayon/s, paper/s, book/s

Week 2 Prompt

Can you spell the word ______________? It starts with the letter _____.

WORD BANK: table, chair, bed, sofa, lamp, door, window, house
t, c, b, s, l, d, w, h

Week 3 Prompt

I like to draw pictures of _______________. This is a picture of __________ trees.

WORD BANK: dogs, cats, flowers, fish, babies
twelve, twenty, fifteen, eleven, seventeen

Week 4 Prompt

This is the way I ____________________. That is the way I ____________________.

WORD BANK: brush my teeth, comb my hair, take a shower

Spell Your Name

This activity is really fun for students to try once they've had some practice pronouncing the letters of the alphabet. Write the two sentences below on the chalk/whiteboard or chart paper. Model how to do the activity by writing your name in the blank. Then read the two sentences and spell your name, pointing to each letter as you say it. Then have each student write his/her name on scrap paper and practice saying each letter with a partner. Finally, have each student come to the board, say the sentence with his/her name in the blank, and then spell his/her name aloud for the class.

My name is _________________.

This is how to spell my name.

PARTNER VERSION

My partner is __________________.

This is how to spell his/her name.

Realia Activity

This is a fun way to help students develop background knowledge and connect key points to be learned with objects they can see/touch. First, pick out a few objects that relate to the word or idea to be presented. Have students pass the objects around, using as many of their five senses as possible to connect with them. Pick out one of the objects that can be tossed and have students toss it around the room. Whoever catches it has to say a word/idea that relates to that object. On the following day, have students bring in and present their own objects that relate to that idea or concept. So, for an example, if the class is learning about transportation vocabulary, the teacher might bring in some toy cars, trucks, airplanes, and a bike. After allowing students to manipulate these objects, take one of the small car toys and toss it to a student who then must name another transportation vocabulary word. Continue this toss game until everyone has had a turn. Finally, students will bring their own transportation objects to share and present during the next class.

Language Experience Activity (LEA)

Provide some sort of interesting topic/activity for the students to generate a discussion using the vocabulary provided in this guide. The teacher should generate the first two sentences by referencing structure and vocabulary examples that have been hung around the room on chart paper; it is important to model these two examples for the class. After the activity, initiate a discussion about the activity where all students contribute. Then have the students dictate sentences about the activity in round-robin style while the teacher writes the sentences on chart paper. The class reads the sentences aloud together and then individuals can read the sentences aloud or pairs can read the sentences to each other.

Word Splash!

In this activity, write a theme word in the middle of chart paper with other vocabulary words around it that all relate to the theme word in the center. Students must then pick a vocabulary word on the chart paper and guess at its meaning. To make an educated guess, students should use any prior knowledge that they have of the vocabulary word, context clues in the sentence with the word, and the fact that the vocabulary word relates to the theme word. It is best if the teacher models this process first with a few examples. Also, students can work in pairs to share their ideas before they present them to the class; this can minimize anxiety over incorrect guesses. This activity works particularly well with the vocabulary cards (Appendix C); see abbreviated example below.

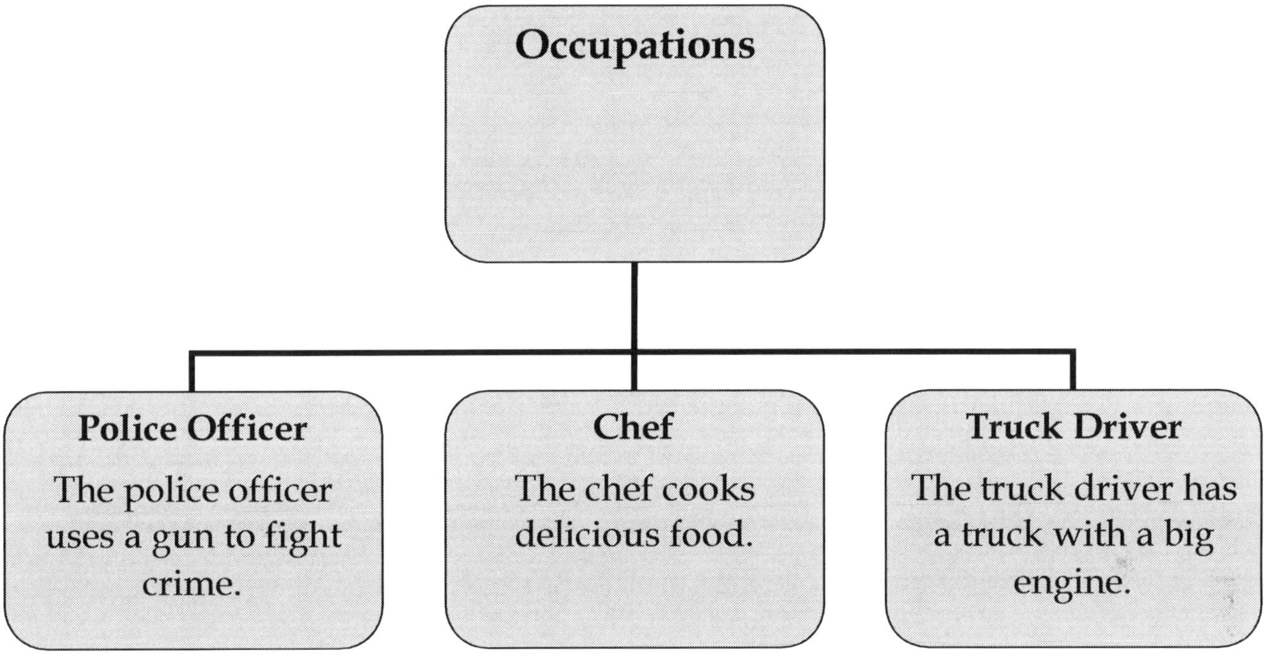

For best results, follow the bulleted steps below to facilitate Word Splash! with the class:

- Go over these directions carefully with the class: pairs pick a work and use cognate/context clues and the theme word to guess at meaning, then students describe meaning.
- Teacher models directions above with the hardest word on chart paper.
- Then teacher assigns a word to each pair of students and gives them a few minutes to talk through its meaning.
- Finally each pair of students describes their word's meaning using one of these sentence stems:
  - The meaning of ______________________ is ______________________.
  - A ______________________ is a tool to ______________________.
  - The definition of a ______________________ is ______________________.

Funky Phrases

For this activity, put students in medium-sized groups. Give each group an envelope of notecards with one word on each notecard; all the notecards in the envelope should make up one complete sentence or question reflecting the grammar structure they are learning. Make sure there is a word for each student in the group; you can do this by labeling the envelopes with the number of words/notecards inside and then forming your student groups based on the number labeled on each envelope. Hand out the envelopes to the groups, and give the groups 5–10 minutes to put their notecards in the right order to make a correct sentence. It is a good idea to model this for the class by picking a few volunteers and showing them how to assemble the words in their envelope into a sentence. Then, one at a time, have individual groups come to the front of the room and arrange themselves in their correct sentence order, with each student in the group holding up one of the notecards so that the class can read the sentence. Pick another student (i.e., one who is not in that group) to read the sentence aloud, and then repeat this assembling process with all of the other groups.

**This activity may not work if you have very young students who are non-readers. In that case, I recommend you try the Quick Sketch Activity instead. It is explained later in this section.*

Observation Walk Activity

In this activity, the teacher takes the students on a walk around the school grounds and points out objects whose names students are learning in their vocabulary lessons for that week. The teacher can chatter away in English during the walk, just letting students hear the authentic sound of the language. Then, every few minutes, the teacher should stop to point out, pronounce, and have students repeat the name of an object. After about every five objects, it's good to say/pantomime a sentence about that object, having students repeat it and try to understand the sentence. This is a fun and stimulating activity; its focus is mostly on the stimulation of letting students stretch their legs while applying English to their surroundings. For the last few minutes of the walk, you might ask students to try naming some of the objects they see in English.

Tommy leads an Observation Walk.

Quick Sketch Activity

This activity is a fun way for students to draw their knowledge of English concepts. For this activity, use the vocabulary cards (Appendix C) that match the theme of the lesson. First, the teacher tells the students what vocabulary word they should draw by saying, "I have a *(vocabulary word)* card." Then the teacher describes the word in a few short, simple sentences, emphasizing quantity, if possible. While the teacher is describing the word, the students try to draw and color the word. For example, the teacher might say, "The *(vocabulary word)* is a place. It has water and sand. The water is blue, and the sand is white. There are six black fish in the water." After repeating these steps a few times with different vocabulary cards, have students trade drawings. Then have each student stand and describe a picture that another student has drawn. It is best to have a sentence about this written on chart paper that students can refer to when composing their sentence—for example, "I have the drawings of *(Carmen)*. There is/are *(a harbor)*."

Kinesthetic Practice Activity

This is a fabulous TPR activity to get students moving as they practice some common prepositions. Before starting this activity, it is good to introduce these words to students by writing the following location prepositions on chart paper and showing students their meanings: on/at/in, near/far from, before/after, below/above, beside. Also, write on chart paper and review the command "Sit ______ your desk." The teacher then gives the class the "sit" command, filling in the blank each time with a different preposition from the list above. Students must then act out that command. Next, make this activity a bit more challenging by using commands with body parts and the same prepositions (see the examples below). After students get the hang of this, let each student take a turn giving a "sit" command for the class to follow.

A Few "Sit" Command Examples

Sit on your desk.

Sit at your desk.

Sit near your desk.

Sit in the seat after your desk.

Sit far from your desk.

Sit below your desk.

A Few More Challenging Body Part Command Examples

Put your arm in your desk.

Put your arm near your desk.

Put your leg below your desk.

Student Questionnaire

Have students make a chart on their papers like the one below. On the left side of the chart, they should write QUESTION, and on the right side, they should write ACTIVITY. Have the class brainstorm various activity questions they can ask each other using whatever grammar structure they are learning that week. The teacher should write their questions on the board, and then students can copy the questions onto the QUESTION side of their chart. Once students have all of their questions ready, have them circulate about the classroom, asking each other the questions. Once they get an affirmative answer to their chart question from another student, they can write that student's name in an affirmative sentence on the ACTIVITY side of their chart, to the right of the question (see example that follows). It is important that the teacher models this process first for the class because the directions are a bit complicated and can seem confusing to students. Then, once everyone has finished and their charts are complete, students can read an affirmative sentence from their charts to the class to share information about their classmates.*_If you work with very young students who are non-readers, you may need to modify this activity in the following way. Instead of having students make/copy their own charts, they should use the class-generated one that the teacher has written on the board. Choose one student at a time to come to the front of the class and pick a partner to whom he/she would like to ask a chart question. Students who know/remember what question they want to ask can go ahead. The teacher may need to review some of the questions with students who aren't sure which question they want to ask and then encourage them to choose one. After the partner answers the question, the student should read the affirmative sentence to the class in order to share the information about the partner._

Question	Activity
Do you walk to school?	Jamie walks to school.
Do you eat pizza?	Spock eats pizza.
Last year, did you look for books in the library?	Last year, Kirk looked for books in the library.
Did you wait at the bus station?	Khan waited at the bus station
Last week, did you go to church?	Last week, Sulu went to church.

Guess It!

In this activity, a student acts out an activity or feeling vocabulary card (Appendix C) while the rest of the class tries to guess what activity or feeling the acting student is doing or feeling. The teacher can start this activity by writing the following on chart paper:

The/A/An <u>(boy, girl, student, students, etc.)</u> is/are ________ing.

OR

The/A/An <u>(boy, girl, student, students, etc.)</u> is/are feeling ______________.

Next, the teacher should model an example of the activity/feeling by having a student or multiple students select and act out one or more of the vocabulary cards while the teacher says the chart paper sentence and inserts the appropriate article and then the student's vocabulary card word in the sentence. Then select another student(s) to pick a card and act out its activity/feeling. Engage the entire class in the activity by having students raise their hands to guess the activity/feeling or by having students guess in a round-robin style. Hand the student who guessed at the action/feeling (correctly or incorrectly) the stack of vocabulary cards so that he/she can select the next card and act it out for the class.

Video Clip Activity

This activity is really helpful in engaging students because it gives them something new and interesting on which to practice or apply their newly learned language concepts. When using video clips, it is important to keep them short (under 1 minute) and to pick clips that highlight the concept you want students to practice. Video clips can be shared with the volume off if the language is overwhelming or doesn't match the concept the teacher is trying to convey. Conversely, the video volume can be turned on if it uses simple language that reinforces the target concept. Sources for videos can be found all over the Web; just google "short video" and the language concept you are highlighting for that day/lesson and then take your pick! My personal favorite free video source is www.pbslearningmedia.org. Here are the steps to follow when using a video clip with students:

- Introduce the video clip with a quick review/preview of the language concept(s) you want students to pay attention to.
- Write a few discussion questions on the board or on chart paper for students to read over/think about during the clip. Here are some examples:
  - What objects/actions/feelings/etc. in the video did you see that match the vocabulary words we have been using?
  - What grammar structure(s) did you hear as the characters/narrator were/was speaking?
  - What did you like about the video clip?
  - What did you dislike about the video clip?
  - What was confusing in the video clip?
  - What did you learn in the video clip?
- Show the video clip.
- Have a 10-minute discussion about the video using the discussion questions to guide the class.

Some Review Topic Examples to Reinforce Through Video Clips

- *To be* present-tense verbs
- Greetings
- Pronouns
- The alphabet; how to spell your name
- *Can* verb structure
- Common phrases about not understanding English
- Demonstratives structure
- *This/that/these/those*

- Present-tense verb structure
- Numbers 1–20
- Birthdays
- Present-continuous-tense verb structure
- Days of the week
- Plurals structure
- *To have*/*to go*/*to do* present-tense verbs
- Commands structure

We watched many video clips of *The Electric Company* (great show for teaching beginning English) from this trusty, old laptop in 2014. Our technology budget in schools is not always sufficient, but we make do.

Appendix I: Games

Games are such a motivating and engaging way for students to practice their language skills in a no-pressure environment. Below are some of my favorite language games.

Numbers Bingo

Hand out blank bingo cards (Appendix J) and have students fill in the numbers 1–20 (they'll have to repeat a few numbers) in any mixed-up order on their card. Students can use beans or pebbles as game pieces. First, read out each letter/number (bingo letter and number in bingo column). Second, repeat the letter/number. Third, give students about 10 seconds to find the letter/number on their bingo card. Finally, write the letter/number that was called out on the chalk/whiteboard or chart paper, so students can check their English and also check that they have placed a bean/pebble on the correct spot. The first student to get five beans/pebbles placed in a row/column calls out "BINGO" and wins a prize. After someone wins, have students clear their cards of game pieces and start again. Collect the bingo cards after the game to be handed out again for the next game.

Letters Bingo

Hand out blank bingo cards (Appendix J) and have students fill in 24 alphabet letters in any mixed-up order on their card. Students can use beans or pebbles as game pieces. First, read out each letter pair (bingo letter and letter in bingo column). Second, repeat the letter pair. Third, give students about 10 seconds to find the letter pair on their bingo card. Finally, write the letter pair that was called out on the chalk/whiteboard or chart paper, so students can check their English and also check that they have placed a bean/pebble on the correct spot. The first student to get five beans/pebbles placed in a row/column calls out "BINGO" and wins a prize. After someone wins, have students clear their cards of game pieces and start again. Collect the bingo cards after the game to be handed out again for the next game.

Simon Says

In this game, the leader (can be teacher or student) gives different commands to the class. Before the game, the teacher can write/review several basic commands relating to the week's lessons and point to them as she/he speaks to help students with comprehension during the game. Also, repeat each command at least twice. At the start of the game, everyone should be standing. If the leader says a command preceded by "Simon says…" then the class can follow that command. But, if the leader only says the command (without saying "Simon says…" first), then the students should not follow the command; anyone who does is out of the game and must sit down.

This and That

All students stand, and the leader (can be teacher or student) names school objects in the classroom, preceded by the word *this* for objects located close to the group or *that* for objects located far from the group. The student must point down (*this*) or point out (*that*) depending on whether the leader says *this* or *that* to name the objects. Students who point incorrectly must sit down. The student left standing is the winner.

This/That/These/Those

Follow the same procedures as in the "This and That" game, but also use the words *these* and *those* to name groups of objects. The student left standing is the winner.

Name It!

Use sticky notes to cover the words on the vocabulary cards (Appendix C), leaving the picture uncovered. Then place the cards face down, with students sitting in a circle around the cards. Allow each student to choose a card and pronounce the name of the object shown on the card in English. If the student does this correctly, he/she can take off the sticky note and keep the card. The student with the most cards at the end of the game is the winner.

Pick the Right Verb!

After teaching or reviewing the present-tense structure, put multiple (one to two sentences for each student in the class) present-tense sentences on chart paper with an *s* and non-*s* choice of the verb to pick for each sentence. In round-robin fashion, let each student read a sentence aloud and pick which verb he/she thinks correctly fits the sentence. Give one point to each student who correctly chooses a verb. Once all sentences have been read, the student with the most points wins the game and earns a prize. To make this game easier, the students can play in pairs. For a more advanced version of this game, have students explain why they picked their verb.

Examples of Sentences

1. Josh arrive/arrives at school on time.
2. They eat/eats dinner at 8:00.
3. I play/plays after school.
4. We play/plays after school.
5. She get/gets up at 6:00.
6. Do/Does he eat fish?
7. I do/does not go to school.

For best results, follow the numbered steps below to play this game with the class:

- Write the game instructions and a long list of present-tense sentences (one to two for each student) on chart paper with the verbs in a different color than the rest of the sentence.
- Have a student read/translate the following game instructions while the teacher models each instruction:
  - Read the sentence silently.
  - Decide which colored verb correctly goes with the pronoun.

  - Read the sentence aloud with the correct colored verb to earn a point.
  - The student with the most points at the end is the winner.
- If the student reads his/her sentence with the correct verb, the teacher gives that student a bean to represent the point earned and has the student circle his/her verb choice on the chart paper so everyone can see. If the student reads his/her sentence with the incorrect verb, the teacher circles the correct verb and explains why it is correct (or has another student do this step).

Spelling Bee

For this game, choose a student to stand at the front of the class. The teacher chooses a vocabulary word card (Appendix C) and reads the vocabulary word to the student. If the student can spell the word out loud by correctly pronouncing each letter of the word for the class without looking at the card, he/she earns two points and can have another card to try to spell. If the student needs to see the card and then correctly pronounces each letter when spelling the word out loud to the class, the student earns one point but does not get a second turn *(you may want to modify this rule if you work with very young students).* Let all students who volunteer have a turn. The student with the most points at the end of the game wins a prize.

English students in Mozambique play a game during English Club.

Appendix J: Bingo Card

B	I	N	G	O
		FREE SPACE ☺		

Appendix K: Word Wall Games

Games with word walls are a great way to practice language concepts learned! A word wall is exactly what it sounds like: one wall (or more) of your classroom devoted to the main words you are using with your students in your lessons. It is important not to overwhelm students, so only put up a few words on the wall every day or so and then spend some time going over the meanings as you display them. I find it works best to write each word in large black letters on an index card, pronounce it for the students, have them repeat its pronunciation, and discuss its definition using TPR/pictures/charades or some other engaging way of explanation (see Appendix Q for some additional suggestions). Then refer to it as often as possible when you sing, read aloud, play games, etc. Below are some of my favorite word wall games.

Suffix It!

Students pick a word on the word wall and add an ending to it. This game works best if you brainstorm all the types of endings that students have learned (plurals, present-continuous "*–ing*", past "*–ed*", etc.) and then write the list of endings on the board. If a student is able to say the word with its ending, he/she gets one point. If a student can say it and write it on the board correctly, he/she gets two points.

It's Your Future

Toss a ball around the classroom. Each student who gets the ball must use a word from the word wall in a future sentence or question. Then that student tosses the ball to someone else.

Opposites

With all students standing, have a student say a word from the word wall and then have the next student say the opposite of that word. If the answering student is correct, he/she gets a point and gets to give someone else a word to say the opposite of. If the student is incorrect, he/she is "out" and must sit down.

You Can Act!

Students get into teams, and one student from each team acts out a word from the word wall for the team. If the student's team can guess the word by using it in a present-tense sentence or question, they get a point and get another try. For example, if the student picks and acts out the word "dog," then the team would have to say something like, "The student is a dog" or "Are you a dog?" or "He is a dog" in order to earn their point. If the student's team is not able to guess the word or use a correct present-tense sentence or question to express the word, the other team gets their turn. You can do a variation on this game by having students draw the words for their team instead of acting them out.

Mystery Word

One student stands outside the classroom while the class decides on a mystery word from the word wall. Then the student outside comes back in and goes to the word wall and stands against it with his/her back to the wall. The standing student must try to guess it by asking the class questions using the correct article (*a* or *an*) in their questions (for example, "Is it a car?" Or "Does it have an ear?"). Once the student guesses the word, he/she can choose another student to guess a new mystery word.

Cross-Out Relay

Divide the class into two teams and write equally difficult word wall words on chart paper, one for each student on the teams. The teams then work to define each word, one student at a time. Once the student whose turn it is has defined the word correctly, the teacher will let the student cross it off the list, and the next student on that team tries to define the next word, and so on. The first team with all words crossed out wins.

It's a New Word!

Each student selects a word from the word wall and makes a new word out of it by changing just one letter in the word. Students get one point for only adding or subtracting an s to change plurality; students get two points for adding or subtracting a letter that changes the meaning of the word. After every student has had a few tries, the student with the most points wins. You can also make this into a relay by grouping students into four groups and having them write their name/old word/new word on one relay group paper. The group with the most new words after a timed interval wins!

Line Up

Divide the class into two lines. The teacher picks a word wall word, and the two students who are first in each line must compete to define it. The student that first defines the word correctly wins, while the other student goes to the end of the line. The next student then competes against the winner. If possible, repeat until everyone in both lines has had a turn.

Stand and Deliver

The teacher reads from the student-created dialogues and students stand (and then sit down quickly) every time the teacher reads a word wall word. This can also be played using the songs (just sing very slowly) instead of the dialogues.

Missing in Action

Have students close their eyes while you remove an action word from the word wall. The student who can act out the word that is missing wins a point. Repeat until someone earns a set number of points.

Observations

Have students use the word *there* in sentences to speak about their observations of the word wall. For example, students might say "there are five words about animals" or "there is no word about planes".

Word!

Have students use word wall words to make past-tense sentences by including *was* or *were* in the sentence. This game can be modified slightly to give students practice making past-tense sentences with past-tense verbs by asking them to combine word wall words with past-tense verbs other than *was/were*. The game can be further modified to make present-tense sentences by asking students to combine word wall words with present-tense verbs.

Locate It

Students must use prepositions of location (*near/far from/before/after/below/above/beside*) to speak about two word wall words' spatial relation to each other. For example, a student might say, "the word *dog* is near the word *cat"* or "the word *run* is not above the word *play*".

Stephanie does a word wall game with a class in Bolivia.

Appendix L: Structures

Structures are best used in the beginning stage of teaching a new English language concept because they provide clear-cut rules that students can memorize and refer to in learning. To avoid confusion for students, I recommend teaching the verb-tense structures with positive, negative, and questioning parts in chunked lessons; sometimes it is best to divide these multi-part structures into three different lessons: one lesson for positive statements, a second lesson for negative statements, and a final lesson for questions in that structure. Other simpler structures or structures that repeat from previously taught topics can be taught in one lesson.

Here are some tips to teach the following structures:

- Write the rule and examples on chart paper or on the board.

- Discuss the rules above the structure chart with the class. Use pantomiming, pictures, and student explanation as much as possible to keep everyone attentive and engaged. For example, when I go over the rule for the pronouns structure, I have students point to someone/something representing each structure by saying, *point to a "he," point to an "it," point to "we,"* etc.

- Read each row of the structure chart aloud while students listen for pronunciation, then have students repeat after you, one row at a time.

- Have each student read an example slowly in round-robin fashion while another student points that example out, if possible, on the corresponding row of the structure chart.

- Finally, play a quick game to give students independent practice with the structure. For example, throw a ball to each student while saying a pronoun and have the student who catches the ball make a sentence or question with that pronoun/corresponding verb using the grammar structure rule. Here are some other game ideas:

  -Sing It: Show and sing lyrics from one of the songs that students have learned; students must stand every time they hear the grammar structure that the class has just learned.

  -Basketball: To take a shot at throwing a small ball in the trash can, students have to give a question form of the grammar structure the class is studying.

  -Unscramble: Give groups of students cards for all the words in a structure's sentence or question; the groups then have to work together to put the cards in order to make a correct sentence/question.

- For further written practice, have students write some statements/questions using each type of pronoun and a few named nouns to substitute for the pronouns. Students can then share their sentences with the class.

**For very young students, you may need to read/chant all rows of the structure, giving students a chance to repeat after you multiple times, rather than having students read on their own. This same process may need to be used for the examples. Moreover, you may need to omit the writing part of this.*

Pronouns Structure

Rules: Pronouns can represent people, places, or things.

- *I/he/she/it* are singular pronouns.
- *We/they* are plural pronouns.
- *You* can be a plural or singular pronoun.

Pronoun, Singular (🕴)	**Pronoun, Plural (🕴 🕴 …… 🕴)**	**Verb**	**+ Rest of Sentence**
I/you		say	the correct answer.
He/she/it		says	the incorrect answer.
	We/they/you	say	no answer!

Examples:

I say the correct answer.
You say the correct answer.
He says the incorrect answer.
They say no answer!
You (all) say no answer!
I sleep in my bed.
(The ice) It melts fast.
(Sam and I) We write slowly.

Present-Tense Structure: "To Be"

Rules: Use this structure to show a state of being, whether it is permanent or temporary.

- Positive sentences
  - For *I*, we use *am* as the main verb.
  - For *he/she/it*, we use *is* as the main verb.
  - For *we/you/they*, we use *are* as the main verb.
- Negative sentences
  - For negatives, we add the negative word *not* after the *to be* verb.
- Questions
  - For questions, we place the *to be* verb at the beginning of the sentence.

	Verb	**Subject/Pronoun**	**+ Verb**	**(Negative)**	**+ Rest of Sentence**
+		I	am		a girl.
		He/she/it	is		sick.
		We/you/they	are		fast.
–		I	am	not	a girl.
		He/she/it	is	not	sick.
		We/you/they	are	not	fast.
?	Am	I			a girl?
	Is	he/she/it			sick?
	Are	we/you/they			fast?

Examples:

Is he frustrated?
We are not miserable.
The dog is sick.
They are brothers.

W & H Questions Structure: Who, What, Where, Why, When (and How…)

Rules: Each question word is used to start a certain type of question. They follow the basic pattern:

Question word + verb + subject (noun or pronoun) + rest of sentence

FUNCTION	SENTENCE STRUCTURE			
Function of Question Word	**Question Word**	**+ Verb**	**+ Pronoun/Noun**	**+ Rest of Sentence**
Asks for information about the noun/pronoun	What	are	you	doing?
Asks for a reason	Why	is	the desk	cold?
Asks about time	When	can	I	use the pencil?
Asks about place or location	Where	is	the crayon?	
Asks what noun/pronoun	Who	am	I?	
Asks about condition or quality	How	are	you?	
Asks about age	How old	is	Steve?	

Examples:

What are you doing?
Why is the desk cold?
When can I use the pencil?
Where is the crayon?
Who am I?
How are you?
Where is the chair?
Who rides the bus to school?
When does school start?
Why is the paper here?
How old is Mary?

Irregular Present-Tense Structure: "To Do"

Rules: This structure is used like all present-tense structures: when the action is general, when the action happens regularly or all the time, or when the statement is always true.

- Positive sentences
  - For *he/she/it*, we add *es* to the main verb.
  - For *I/we/you/they*, we don't add *es* to the main verb.
  - We don't use helping verbs in positive sentences.
- Negative sentences
  - For *he/she/it*, add the helping verb *does* + *not* + main verb *do*.
  - For *I/we/you/they*, add the helping verb *do* + *not* + main verb *do*.
- Questions
  - For *he/she/it*, add the helping verb *does* + pronoun + main verb *do* as the first word in the sentence.
  - For *I/we/you/they*, add the helping verb *do* + pronoun + main verb *do* as the first word in the sentence.

	(Question Word)	**Subject/Pronoun**	**(Negative)**	**+ Verb/s**	**+ Rest of Sentence**
+		I/we/you/they		do go	crossword puzzles. to school.
		He/she/it		does goes	crafts on Sunday. on Friday.
–		I/we/you/they	do not	do go	crossword puzzles. to school.
		He/she/it	does not	do go	crafts on Sunday. on Friday.
?	Do	I/we/you/they		do go	crossword puzzles? to school?
	Does	he/she/it		do go	crafts on Sunday? on Friday?

Examples:

I do crossword puzzles.
She does crafts on Sunday.
I do not do crossword puzzles.

It does not do crafts on Sunday.
Do they do crossword puzzles?
Do John and Jenny do crossword puzzles?

Irregular Present-Tense Structure: "To Go"

Rules: This structure is used like all present-tense structures: when the action is general, when the action happens regularly or all the time, or when the statement is always true.

- Positive sentences
  - For *he/she/it*, we add *es* to the main verb.
  - For *I/we/you/they*, we don't add *es* to the main verb.
  - We don't use helping verbs in positive sentences.
- Negative sentences
  - For *he/she/it*, add the helping verb *does* + *not* + main verb *go*.
  - For *I/we/you/they*, add the helping verb *do* + *not* + main verb *go*.
- Questions
  - For *he/she/it*, add the helping verb *does* + pronoun + main verb *go* as the first word in the sentence.
  - For *I/we/you/they*, add the helping verb *do* + pronoun + main verb *go* as the first word in the sentence.

	(Question Word)	Subject/Pronoun	(Negative)	+ Verb/s	+ Rest of Sentence
+		I/we/you/they		go	to school.
		He/she/it		goes	on Friday.
–		I/we/you/they	do not	go	to school.
		He/she/it	does not	go	on Friday.
?	Do	I/we/you/they		go	to school?
	Does	he/she/it		go	on Friday?

Examples:

I go to the doctor.
She goes to the police.
I do not go to the lawyer.
The painter goes to the store.
The soldier goes to war.
The singer goes to the concert.
The farmer goes to the market.
The maids go to the house.
The janitor does not go to war.
You and the cashier do not go to the store.
Did the astronauts go to space?
It does not go to the telephone.
Do they go to the computer?
Do John and Jenny go home?

Can Structure

Rules: *Can* is used with a second verb to show what is or is not possible. All pronouns use *can* the same way.

- *Can* is followed by a second verb.
- For negatives, we add the negative word *not* (closed up to *can*) between the two verbs (i.e., *cannot*).
- For questions, we place *can* at the beginning of the sentence.

	(Question Word)	Subject/Pronoun	+ Verb	(Negative)	+ Second Verb	+ Rest of Sentence
+		I/we/you/they/he/she/it	can		run	to school.
–		I/we/you/they/he/she/it	can	not	run	to school.
?	Can	I/we/you/they/he/she/it			run	to school?

Examples:

Can Jim (he) have a snack? No, Jim cannot have a snack.
Can you and I (we) go to the park? No, you and I cannot go to the park.
Can you help me? Yes, I can help you.
Can Sue and Rosa (they) attend the show? Yes, Sue and Rosa can attend the show.

Demonstratives Structure

Rules: Use *this/these* for close objects; use *that/those* for far objects.

CLOSE Object/s	+ Verb	+ Rest of Sentence
This	is	a pen.
These	are	books.

FAR Object/s	+ Verb	+ Rest of Sentence
That	is	a pen.
Those	are	books.

Examples:

This is a bee.
That is a tree.
Those are sweaters.
These are kids.

Present-Tense Structure

Rules: Use this structure when the action is general, when the action happens regularly or all the time, or when the statement is always true.

- Positive sentences
  - For *he/she/it*, we add *s* to the main verb.
  - For *I/we/you/they*, we don't add *s* to the main verb.
  - We don't use helping verbs in positive sentences.
- Negative sentences
  - For *he/she/it*, add the helping verb *does* + *not* + main verb.
  - For *I/we/you/they*, add the helping verb *do* + *not* + main verb.
- Questions
  - For *he/she/it*, add the helping verb *does* + pronoun + main verb as the first word in the sentence.
  - For *I/we/you/they*, add the helping verb *do* + pronoun + main verb as the first word in the sentence.

	(Question Word)	Subject/Pronoun	(Negative)	+ Verb/s	+ Rest of Sentence
+		I/we/you/they		run	to school.
		He/she/it		runs	fast.
–		I/we/you/they	do not	run	to school.
		He/she/it	does not	run	fast.
?	Do	I/we/you/they		run	to school?
	Does	he/she/it		run	fast?

Examples:

We run to school in August.
Sam and I (we) write slowly.
Do Sam and I write slowly?
Sam and I do not write slowly.
The brothers run to school.
Jenny and John (they) talk a lot.
Do Mother and Father talk a lot?

The husband and wife do not talk a lot.
I sleep in my bed.
It runs fast.
We do not run to school.
She does not run fast.
Do you run to school?
Does he run fast?
The ice (it) melts fast.

Present-Continuous Structure

Rules: This structure is for actions that are happening right now/close to right now or for actions in the future.

- Positive sentences
  - For *he/she/it*: subject/pronoun + helping verb *is* + main verb + *ing* + rest of sentence
  - For *I*: subject/pronoun + helping verb *am* + main verb + *ing* + rest of sentence
  - For *we/you/they*: subject/pronoun + helping verb *are* + main verb + *ing* + rest of sentence
- Negative sentences
  - For *he/she/it*: subject/pronoun + helping verb *is* + *not* + main verb + *ing* + rest of sentence
  - For *I*: subject/pronoun + helping verb *am* + *not* + main verb + *ing* + rest of sentence
  - For *we/you/they*: subject/pronoun + helping verb *are* + *not* + main verb + *ing* + rest of sentence
- For questions, switch the order of the subject/pronoun and helping verb.

	(Question Word)	**Subject/ Pronoun**	**Helping Verb**	**(Helping Verb with Negative)**	**+ Verb + "–*ing*"**	**+ Rest of Sentence**
+		I	am		cooking	now.
		He/she/it	is		exercising	tomorrow.
		We/you/they	are		saying	the answer.
–		I	am	not	cooking	now.
		He/she/it	is	not	exercising	tomorrow.
		We/you/they	are	not	saying	the answer.
?	Am	I			cooking	now?
	Is	he/she/it			exercising	tomorrow?
	Are	we/you/they			saying	the answer?

Examples:

I am cooking now.
We are saying the answer.

She is not eating tomorrow.
Is it showing tomorrow?

Irregular Present-Tense Structure: "To Have"

Rules: This structure is used like all present-tense structures: when the action is general, when the action happens regularly or all the time, or when the statement is always true.

- Positive sentences
  - For *he/she/it*, we replace *ve* with *s* at the end of the main verb.
  - For *I/we/you/they*, we don't add *s* to the main verb.
  - We don't use helping verbs in positive sentences.
- Negative sentences
  - For *he/she/it*, add the helping verb *does* + *not* + main verb.
  - For *I/we/you/they*, add the helping verb *do* + *not* + main verb.
- Questions
  - For *he/she/it*, add the helping verb *does* + pronoun + main verb as the first word in the sentence.
  - For *I/we/you/they*, add the helping verb *do* + pronoun + main verb as the first word in the sentence.

	(Question Word)	**Subject/Pronoun**	**(Negative)**	**+ Verb/s**	**+ Rest of Sentence**
+		I/we/you/they		have	a keyboard.
		He/she/it		has	a printer.
–		I/we/you/they	do not	have	a keyboard.
		He/she/it	does not	have	a printer.
?	Do	I/we/you/they		have	a keyboard?
	Does	he/she/it		have	a printer?

Examples:

I have a thermometer.
Sam and I (we) have watches.
Does it have a video camera?
Sam and I do not have a video camera.

The brother has a fax.
Jenny and John (they) have a computer.
Do Mother and Father have a photocopier?
The husband has a calculator.

Plurals Structure

Rule #1: For most words, just add *s*.

Singular (1)	Plural (2, 3, 4,...10+)
computer	computers
keyboard	keyboards
printer	printers

Rule #2: For words ending in *s, x, z, ch*, or *sh*, add *es*.

Singular (1)	Plural (2, 3, 4,...10+)
watch	Watches
bush	Bushes
fax	Faxes
glass	glasses

Rule #3: For some words, the word totally changes.

Singular (1)	Plural (2, 3, 4,...10+)
child	children
person	people
tooth	teeth
foot	feet
mouse	mice

Rule #4: For some words, the plural and singular forms are the same.

Singular (1)	Plural (2, 3, 4,...10+)
deer	deer
fish	fish
sheep	sheep

Commands Structure

Before starting this activity, it is best to teach the *on/at/in* prepositions by writing them on chart paper and showing students their meanings: *on* indicates surface, *in* indicates an enclosed space, and *at* indicates a point. Here's an example of how to show students the meaning of *on*: the teacher takes a pencil, puts it on the table, and says "the pencil is on the table," while pointing to the word *on* on the chart paper. After showing students the meanings, the teacher should say the word, have students repeat the word, and then have individual students pronounce the word. Finally, the teacher should point to and say a simple sentence about the prepositions (for example, "put the pencil at the door," "put the pencil on the table," etc.) and give each student a chance to move the pencil based on the preposition statement.

Rule: Commands take the infinitive or *to* form of the verb—just don't forget to drop the *to*!

(Negative)	+ Verb	+ Rest of Sentence (with in/on/at preposition)
(Do not)	sit	down **in** the chair.
(Do not)	stand	up **on** the floor.
(Do not)	turn	left/right **at** the sign.
(Do not)	write	your first name **on** the paper.
(Do not)	put	your hand **in** your pocket.
(Do not)	put	your hand **on** your head.
(Do not)	say	your name **at** the door.

Examples:

Sit down in the car.
Do not sit down in the chair.
Stand up!
Do not stand up on the bus!
Turn the van left at the sign.
Do not turn right on your bike.
Do not write your name on the skateboard.
Put your hand on the motorcycle.
Do not raise your hand.
Say your name at the door.

Possessive Adjectives Structure

Rules: Possessive adjectives show who/what owns something.

- *My/his/her/its* are singular possessive adjectives.
- *Our/their* are plural possessive adjectives.
- *Your* can be a plural or singular possessive adjective.
- Possessive adjectives can occur at the beginning, middle, or end of a sentence/question.

Pronoun or Noun	Verb	Singular Possessive Adjective (🚹)	Plural Possessive Adjective (🚹 🚹 …… 🚹)	+ Rest of Sentence
I	raise	my		arm.
You	raise	your		eyebrows.
He	raises	his		hand.
She	raises	her		shoulder.
It	raises	its		leg.
We	raise		our	heads.
They	raise		their	fingers.
You (all)	raise		your	hands.

Examples:

I raise my arm.
You raise your eyebrows.
He does not raise his eyebrows.
Did it raise its leg?
Our arms are tired.
She raises her arms and claps her hands.
My eyes are closed.

English student show off their new dictionaries in Mozambique.

Past-Tense Structure

Rules: Use this structure when an action or habit started and ended in the past.

- Positive sentences
  - For all subjects/pronouns (*I/we/you/they/he/she/it*), we add "*–ed*" to the end of the main verb.
  - There are many irregular forms of past-tense verbs where we don't add "*–ed*".
  - The suffix "*–ed*" is pronounced differently with different verbs: sometimes as a /t/ sound, a /d/ sound, or an /ed/ sound.
  - We don't use helping verbs in positive sentences.
- Negative sentences
  - For all subjects/pronouns (*I/we/you/they/he/she/it*), add the helping verb *did* + *not* + main verb.
- Questions
  - For all subjects/pronouns (*I/we/you/they/he/she/it*), add the helping verb *did* + subject/pronoun + main verb as the first word in the sentence.

	(Question Word)	**Subject/Pronoun**	**(Negative)**	**+ Verb/s + "*–ed*"**	**+ Rest of Sentence**
+		I/we/you/they/he/she/it		walked	to school.
–		I/we/you/they/he/she/it	did not	walk	fast.
?	Did	I/we/you/they/he/she/it		walk	to school?

Examples:

Uncle Jim snored in bed.
It snored a lot.
We did not walk to school in November.
She did not walk fast.
Did you walk to school?
Did Aunt Jane walk fast?

The ice (it) melted fast.
Did it melt fast last December?
It did not melt fast in July.
Sam and I (we) jumped slowly.
Did Sam and I jump slowly?
Sam and I did not jump slowly.

Articles Structure

Rules:

- An article is an adjective that always goes before a noun to give some information about it.
- *A/An* (indefinite articles) always go with singular nouns and refer to any item—an indefinite or general item.
- *A* is for words that start with a consonant; *an* is for words that start with a vowel (a, e, i, o, u).
- *The* (definite article) can go with singular or plural nouns but refers to a particular or definite item.
- Count nouns are nouns that can be counted, such as stores, churches, and arms.
- Non-count nouns are nouns that cannot be counted, such as water or English. Non-count nouns never follow *a/an* but sometimes follow *the*.
- We don't use articles with names, pronouns, demonstratives (this, that, these, those).

Singular (1)			**Plural (2, 3, 4,…10+)**	
Definite Article	**Indefinite Article**	**Noun**	**Definite Article**	**Nouns**
the	—	store	the	stores
—	a	church	—	—
—	an	airport	—	—

Examples:

The bank is in the city.
A bank is in the city.
The banks are in Austin.
An office is big.

The offices are big.
The water is in the library.
~~A~~ water is in the library.

There Structure

Rule: *There* is used to indicate that something exists and can also convey the location of something. *There* can go with a plural or singular subject (rest of sentence) and usually combines with the *to be* verb in most tenses.

- Positive sentences
  - Present tense: *There* is followed by the *to be* verb: *is* (singular)/*are* (plural). The *to be* verb is the main verb.
  - Past tense: *There* is followed by the *to be* verb: *was* (singular)/*were* (plural). The *to be* verb is the main verb.
- Negative sentences
  - For negatives, we add the negative word *no* after the *to be* verb.
- Questions
  - For questions, we place the *to be* verb at the beginning of the sentence.
- For a future lesson: *There* can also go at the end of the sentence to show a location away from you:
  - *Let's go over there.*
  - *The chair is there.*

Present Tense

	(Verb)	**There**	**+ Verb**	**(Negative)**	**+ Rest of Sentence**
+		There (singular = 1)	is		a school.
		There (plural = 2+)	are		seven schools.
–		There (singular = 1)	is	no	school.
		There (plural = 2+)	are	no	schools.
?	Is	there (singular = 1)			a school?
	Are	there (plural = 2+)			schools?

Past Tense

	(Verb)	**There**	**+ Verb**	**(Negative)**	**+ Rest of Sentence**
+		There (singular = 1)	was		a school.
		There (plural = 2+)	were		seven schools.
–		There (singular = 1)	was	no	school.
		There (plural = 2+)	were	no	schools.
?	Was	there (singular = 1)			a school?
	Were	there (plural = 2+)			schools?

Examples:

There are some boys at school.
There are no boys at school.
Are there some boys at school?
There is a girl in the mall.
There are teachers in the school.
There were books in the library.
There was a boat at the port.

Stephanie teaches a class on structures.

Past-Tense Structure: "To Be"

Rules: Use this structure to show a state of being in the past, whether it is permanent or temporary.

- Positive sentences
  - For *I/he/she/it*, we use *was* as the main verb.
  - For *we/you/they*, we use *were* as the main verb.
- Negative sentences
  - For negatives, we add the negative word *not* after the *to be* verb.
- Questions
  - For questions, we place the *to be* verb at the beginning of the sentence.

	Verb	**Subject/Pronoun**	**+ Verb**	**(Negative)**	**+ Rest of Sentence**
+		I/he/she/it	was		sick.
		We/you/they	were		smart.
–		I/he/she/it	was	not	sick.
		We/you/they	were	not	smart.
?	Was	I/he/she/it			sick?
	Were	we/you/they			smart?

Examples:

I was a boy.
Felipe (he) was angry.
We were sick last week.
Was it hungry yesterday?
Sam and I (we) were friends.

Jimmy and John (they) were brothers.
Are you excited?
The bus was yellow.
My favorite color was pink.

Future-Simple-Tense Structure

Rules: Use this structure when the action happens in the near or far future or is a prediction.

- Positive sentences
  - For all subjects/pronouns (*I/we/you/they/he/she/it*), we put *will* before the main verb.
- Negative sentences
  - For all subjects/pronouns (*I/we/you/they/he/she/it*), we put *will not* before the main verb.
- Questions
  - For all subjects/pronouns (*I/we/you/they/he/she/it*), we put *will* as the first word in the sentence before the subject/pronoun.

	(Question Word)	Subject/Pronoun	Auxiliary Verb	(Negative)	+ Verb/s	+ Rest of Sentence
+		I/we/you/they he/she/it	will		run	to school.
–		I/we/you/they he/she/it	will	not	run	to school.
?	Will	I/we/you/they he/she/it			run	to school?

Examples:

We will not run to school.
She will not run with her legs.
Will you run with your eyes open?
Will he open the door with his hands?

The cat will listen with its ears.
Will the cat listen?
We will not wave our arms.

Appendix M: Field Trips

Field trips are a wonderful way to have students apply their language skills in an authentic setting. Having learned a second and third language myself, I know that the best way to learn a language is through immersion, and what better way to immerse your students than to take them on outings away from the classroom where they can practice and hear the language in all of its diverse and natural forms. Below are 11 options for field trips along with corresponding activities that will help your students get the most out of the experience. Each field trip option has an activity explanation that lists English-speaking questions/topics that should be practiced first in the classroom before the field trip. These field trip options can easily be recycled throughout the lessons in this guide. In addition, this field trip list is just a starting point, as I'm sure you will have ideas on other places students can go in your town to practice their English.

Begin the field trip activity by having students work in pairs in the classroom to plan out/practice their activity and what they will say in English during the excursion. Then have students enter establishments in a small group with a means to introduce themselves and their mission right away. For example, they might say, "I am a student of English. I want to practice my English today. Can I speak with you or ask you some questions for 5 minutes?" With the state of heightened security these days in the world, this will help to reassure others that it is safe to talk with your students. If you have a large English class, you may need to break your class into smaller groups and send them to different locations on their own or with an adult chaperone. Finally, it is crucial to meet back together after the field trip as a whole class so the teacher can lead a discussion where students can present and process their field trip experiences. Some of these excursions will be easier to do if you are teaching English in an English-speaking country, but there are many on the list that can be enjoyed in a non-English-speaking country. Although most of these field trip ideas are fine for both children and adults, you might simplify the field trip if you teach younger children.

1. Shop at the grocery store: Take students to a nearby supermarket or food market to pick out and buy a few items. During this excursion, have them communicate with other customers and ask store employees questions.

   *Activity: Have each student write a list of 5–10 items to buy in order to achieve a certain goal (such as baking a cake or mopping the floor). Students must then locate and purchase or record the location of all items on their own, asking at least two employees for help in the process.

2. Visit the U.S. (or another English-speaking) embassy: Take students to the local U.S. embassy where they must talk to three people working there.

   *Activity: Have students generate three questions or conversation topics each (for example, "Where is the bathroom?" or "How do you like working in this embassy?"). Then, at the embassy, they must talk to various employees/visitors there, such as the doorman, bathroom attendant, visiting Americans, etc., to get answers to their questions.

3. Go to a concert: Take the class to a concert where songs will be sung in English. Sing along and converse with other concert-goers to practice English.

   *Activity: Print out the lyrics to some of the songs that will be sung beforehand. Read these lyrics with students, having them learn the songs so they can sing along during the concert.

4. Go to an English language-themed café or restaurant: Take students for a tea to a nearby café or restaurant that has an English theme and is known to be frequented by English speakers.

   *Activity: Have students write out three different topics of conversation concerning current events in the country most frequented in the establishment. Have students introduce themselves and strike up a conversation with an employee or customer. Students can then jot down notes as they talk to people about these conversation topics. Alternately, students can practice ordering food/drinks in English.

5. Visit the library: Take students to the local library and have them enlist help from the librarian to research a topic in English.

   *Activity: Each student should pick a topic that interests him/her and write out some research questions on that topic. Once at the library, students can show their questions to the librarian, using their English to find/write answers to the questions.

6. Use public transportation: Have students take a bus, taxi, or streetcar, using English to describe to the driver where they want to go and getting advice about the best way to get there.

   *Activity: Have students make a list of directional vocabulary words they will need to find their location (for example, right, left, go straight, pass the…, etc.). They can then use this vocabulary to discuss their destination with the driver.

7. Visit a local gym: Have students get information on the gym's equipment, facilities, and workout classes.

   *Activity: Students can prepare a workout goal for themselves and then use that goal to get information or a plan from the gym attendant on what facilities the gym has that can help them achieve their goal.

8. Visit a local tourist information center: Students can ask questions about the city or research popular attractions while at the tourist center.

   *Activity: Have students write out three to five questions about the city they are in and then use their English to converse with the tour center attendant to get answers to their questions.

9. Go to an English movie: Take your class to an English-speaking film where they can compare what they hear with the subtitles, writing down inconsistencies or new slang terms they don't understand or would like to remember.

   *Activity: Have students make a chart on notebook paper with three columns: (1) New Expressions, (2) New Words, and (3) Body Language I Do Not Understand. They can fill in these columns as they watch the movie and then share what they've written during a class discussion after the movie.

10. Take an English bus tour: Take the class on a bus tour designed for English-speaking foreign tourists.

    *Activity: Have students make a list of five things they think the guide will say during the tour (such as "look to the left," etc.) and then check off the ones they hear when they're on the tour.

11. Go on a virtual field trip: Although this option pales in comparison to an actual field trip outside the school, if you have a good computer lab and access to the Internet, this can be a fair alternative if field trips are too difficult or expensive for your class. Below is a good link with lots of virtual field trips: http://www.areavibes.com/library/online-field-trips-for-students/.

We meet all kinds of interesting people and situations when we go on English field trips!

Appendix N: Create Your Own Dialogue

As students advance in their level of English, they no longer need to have premade dialogues that they must follow. At this final level of beginner, students can have fun creating their own dialogues. The best way to facilitate the Create Your Own Dialogue (CYOD) experience is to follow the steps below:

- Show students a pre-written dialogue as an example they can follow, if necessary. An example is below:

  Student A: Hello, is it snowing in the park?

  Student B: Yes, it is snowing. There is usually snow in December.

  Student A: My sister likes the snow.

  Student B: My grandparents liked the snow, too.

- Provide some key words and topics for the CYOD experience by writing the dialogue key words and dialogue topic/title on chart paper and reading through them with the students. In this step, you would also discuss and define any necessary vocabulary (see Appendix Q for ideas). Also, review any verb conjugations and/or grammar structures.
- Model how a group would work together to write and practice their dialogue. You might even brainstorm/write out some sentences/questions for the dialogue.
- Afterward, have pairs or groups write and practice their new dialogue and then present their dialogues to the class.

It usually takes about 10 minutes for student to create the dialogue, 10 minutes to practice it, and 15–30 minutes to present all the dialogues, depending on how large your class is.

**For very young students, just continue with the pre-written two-line dialogues so students can practice by copying your model, rather than by reading. You might also have each student present the dialogue to the class with you as his/her partner because very young students may not be able to practice in unsupervised pairs.*

Possible Topics with Key Words

- Favorite Month of the Year: month/year, favorite, why/what, to like, seasons, summer/winter/spring/fall, holiday/birthday, because
- What I Did Yesterday: yesterday, to do, what, to walk, to look, to jump, to watch, to study, to work, to enjoy, to cook
- Tell About Your Family: family members, who/how many, to have, brother/sister, mother/father, son/daughter, grandma/grandpa, cousin, aunt/uncle
- How You Are Feeling: how, to be, feeling, to feel, sad, happy, sick, tired, hungry, thirsty, angry
- Feelings About School: school, teacher, student, schoolwork, to like, to dislike, embarrassed, anxious, confused, excited, calm
- Your Favorite Movie: favorite, movie, was/is, because, to like, character, plot, setting

- When You Were Younger: was, child, baby, when, to cry, to walk, to study, to play
- Describe Your City: farm, community, park, factory, school, gas station, grocery store, library, road, in/on/at, near/far, there is/are, to have
- A Visit to the Doctor: arm, leg, hand, foot, throat, nose, eye, ear, to go, when, anxious, to hurt, doctor, nurse
- A Walk Through the Community: a walk, to walk, community, in/on/at, be beside, before/after, ranch, cinema, bank, church, post office

Students use vocabulary cards as a resource in Create Your Own Dialogue.

Appendix O: Dialogues

The following dialogues are a great way to facilitate a controlled practice of the concepts/vocabulary students have learned. Discuss and define any necessary vocabulary, verb conjugations, and/or grammar structures. Write the dialogue on chart paper and read through it with the students, with the teacher pronouncing each line of the dialogue first and then the students reading/repeating it chorally. Also, brainstorm/write out some options for the blanks. Afterward, have pairs practice for a few minutes and then have pairs act out their dialogue for the group.

**For very young students, you might have a two-line dialogue so students can practice by copying your model, rather than by reading. You might also have individual students present the dialogue to the class with you as their partner because very young students may not be able to practice in unsupervised pairs.*

Dialogue #1: To Be

Student A: Hello, what is your name?
Student B: My name is ____________. What is your name?
Student A: I am ______________. It is nice to meet you.
Student B: Nice to meet you, too. Goodbye.

Dialogue #2: Greetings

Student A: Hello, how are you?
Student B: I am ______________. How are you?
Student A: I am ______________. Thanks for asking.
Student B: Goodbye.

Dialogue #3: Can I?

Student A: Hello, can I use a pencil?
Student B: Yes, you can, because I have (#) pencils. Can I share your eraser?
Student A: You can share my eraser. Thank you.
Student B: You are welcome.

Dialogue #4: Demonstratives

Student A: Good morning. Do you know what this is?
Student B: Yes, this is a ________________.
Student A: Thanks, that is helpful.
Student B: You are welcome. What are those?
Student A: Those are __________________.
Student B: Thanks, goodbye.

Dialogue #5: Numbers/Birthday

Student A: Today is my birthday!
Student B: Wow, Happy Birthday! How old are you?
Student A: I am ____ years old. How old are you?
Student B: I am ____ years old. How old is your sister/brother?
Student A: She/he is ____ years old. Goodbye!
Student B: See you later!

Stephanie models a clothes dialogue with a student in Masaca, Mozambique.

Appendix P: Stem Conversations

As students advance in their level of English, they no longer need to repeat a set dialogue word for word. At *Volume Two* of the beginner level, they can start to use their own ideas in conversation presentations with stem sentences. The steps for facilitating stem conversations are similar to those used in dialogues.

Discuss and define any necessary vocabulary (use TPR to help students remember vocabulary meanings; see our recommendations section- page x- for a description of TPR, if necessary). Also, review any verb conjugations and/or grammar structures. Write the conversation on chart paper and read through it with the students, pronouncing each line of the conversation for the class and then having the students read/repeat it chorally. Also, brainstorm/write out some options for the blanks. Next, have pairs practice for a few minutes and then have each pair present their conversation for the group.

**For very young students, just continue with the two-line dialogues so students can practice by copying your model, rather than by reading. Each of the conversations below can easily be turned into a dialogue by adding the words students should say and leaving only one-word blanks. You might also have each student present the dialogue to the class with you as his/her partner because very young students may not be able to practice in unsupervised pairs.*

Conversation #1: Present-Continuous Verbs with Plurals and Technology

Explain what you like about technology, using the conversation stems below.

Student A: *(greeting)* ______________________________.
Student B: *(greeting)* ______________________________.
Student A: We are learning about technology vocabulary. My favorite types of technology are:
____.
Student B: I like technology, also. In my house, the technology I have is:
____.
Student A: *(saying goodbye)* ________________________.
Student B: *(saying goodbye)* ________________________.

Conversation #2: Present-Irregular Verbs

Explain an irregular verb that you have learned about to your partner, using the conversation stems below.

Student A: *(greeting)* ______________________________.
Student B: *(greeting)* ______________________________.
Student A: Did you know ___________________ and _________________ are irregular verbs?
Some examples of each verb are:
I ________.
She ______.
Student B: Wow! _______________ and ___________ are also irregular verbs. They sound like:
You _______.
It ________.
Student A: *(saying goodbye)* ________________________.
Student B: *(saying goodbye)* ________________________.

Conversation #3: Commands!

Explain what commands your family or teachers give you, using the conversation stems below.

Student A: *(greeting)* ______________________________.
Student B: *(greeting)* ______________________________.
Student A: Do people give you commands? My mom tells me to
"___________________________!" and "_______________________!"
Student B: Yes! My teacher tells me to "_______________________!" and
"___________________!"
Student A: *(saying goodbye)* ________________________.
Student B: *(saying goodbye)* ________________________.

More advanced students present a stem conversation about clothes in Masaca, Mozambique.

Appendix Q: Read Alouds

At this level, students know enough English to begin to understand and enjoy English easy-reader chapter books. These are books typically written for native English-speaking children who are learning to read in English. Below is a list of excellent easy-reader chapter books that you can read aloud to students learning English at the beginning level. Before reading aloud to students, discuss, define, or review any necessary vocabulary (for strategies, see Appendix Q) or grammar structures that are central to the pages you will be reading that day. You can also put some of these words—perhaps the most common ones—up on your word wall (see Appendix J). Gather students around you on the floor or in chairs and read the book aloud to them, showing them all the pictures and pantomiming actions whenever possible. Read pages slowly and use body cues and facial expressions to help students understand meaning. Whenever possible without losing the flow of the story, take time to point out those vocabulary words in the book that also appear on/in the charts/word banks/songs, etc., that you have hanging on classroom walls. After reading the selection for the day, ask a student to translate the main points read so everyone can understand its meaning. Then have each student verbally answer an oral comprehension question related to the story. Below are some examples of thought-provoking comprehension questions with which to start. In addition, some other ways to actively involve students during read-aloud time are outlined on the next page.

Possible Read-Aloud Titles

Bread and Jam for Frances, by Russell Hoban
The Big Race, by Morgan Matthews
There's a Hippopotamus Under My Bed, by Mike Thaler
I Can Read About Dogs and Puppies, by J. I. Anderson
I Can Read About Reptiles, by David Cutts
In a Dark, Dark Room..., retold by Alvin Schwartz
Two Greedy Bears, by Mirra Ginsburg
Professor Possum's Great Adventure, by Michael Pellowski
Rats on the Roof and Other Stories, by James Marshall
Amelia Bedelia's Family Album, by Peggy Parish
Clifford the Big Red Dog, by Norman Bridwell
Frog and Toad Are Friends, by Arnold Lobel
Amazing Grace, by Mary Hoffman
Amber Brown Is Not a Crayon, by Paula Danzinger
The Magic Tree House Series, by Mary Pope Osbourne
Cam Jansen Series, by David Adler
Flat Stanley Series, by Jeff Brown
The Blue Ghost, by Marion Dane Bauer

Examples of Comprehension Questions

What is the name of this character (point)?
Who is an important character in this story?
Where is the story (taking place/occurring)?
Describe the location of the story.
What is the most exciting event?

When is the story (taking place)?
What did you learn from the story?
Where does the character work or go in the story?
How old is the character?
How many family members/siblings does the character have?
What did the character say?
What is the problem in the story?
What is the solution?
Does the character like _____?
Why is the character *insert emotion word*?

Ways to Actively Involve Students in Read-Aloud Time

- Decide on a signal that, when used, will indicate to students that they should call out an answer or respond to the story at the same time.
- Have students describe to their partner what they see in a certain illustration in the story.
- Have students tell about how a certain event or character in the book is similar to something in their own life.
- Have a student act out the story to the class as the teacher reads aloud.
- Have pairs act out the story to each other as the teacher reads aloud.
- Have students draw events/characters in the story as the teacher reads about them.
- At the end of the read-aloud time, have students close their eyes and imagine the next part of the story.
- Use TPR to have students make motions with their bodies to show what is happening in the story.
- Throughout the read-aloud time, have students show their thumbs—pointing up if they understand what is happening in the story and pointing down if they don't understand the story events.

Appendix R: Strategies for Teaching Vocabulary

Obviously, at this beginning level of English, students will be flooded with new vocabulary. To process and retain all these different words and their meanings, experiencing a word and its definition one time will not do the trick. Therefore, at this early language stage, it is crucial to infuse your lessons with meaningful vocabulary retention activities at every turn. Here are some tips and strategies for doing that:

- Introducing vocabulary for a story, song, or other activity is an invaluable opportunity to take advantage of vocabulary instruction. This is because the students are especially engaged and open to learning because they are excited about a new activity that they haven't done before and that is more interesting and fun than direct instruction or traditional practice.
- When introducing a vocabulary word, the teacher can quickly write the actual sentence or verse showing the vocabulary word in context that will be used in the activity.
- The teacher should pronounce the word for students and then have the class repeat the word.
- The teacher (or another student) can then define the word. Try acting out the word, saying its translation, drawing it on the board, or using some other nontraditional way to show its definition.
- The teacher can then ask for students to briefly share their personal experiences with the vocabulary word.
- Again the class should say the vocabulary word a final time.

Example of Introducing a New Vocabulary Word

- **Teacher:** *Today we will continue reading our book,* Bread and Jam for Frances, *and we have some new words in the story today. One of these new words is SOUP. Here is how it is used in the story:*

  SOUP

  "I have tomato soup."

  Let's all say the word together.
- **Entire class:** *SOUP*
- **Teacher:** *Who can show us or tell us the definition of soup?*
- **Bella:** motions blowing on and eating soup with her hands and mouth
- **Teacher:** *Yes! Anyone else?*
- **Edward:** *Sopa*
- **Teacher:** *Very good. Soup, or sopa, is a liquid food that we eat, usually with a bowl and spoon. Raise your hand if you like to eat soup. What is your favorite kind of soup?*
- **Jacob:** *I like bean soup.*
- **Teacher:** *Great! Let's say the word again to remember it.*
- **Entire class:** *SOUP!*

Appendix S: Bibliography

If you would like to learn more about any of the strategies or activities in this teaching guide, please refer to the sources below.

Area Vibes, http://www.areavibes.com/library/online-field-trips-for-students/.

Asher, James. *Learning Another Language Through Actions.* 7th ed. Los Gatos, CA: Sky Oak Productions, 2009.

Bear, Donald, Lori Helman, Marcia Invernizzi, Shane Templeton, and Francine R. Johnston. *Words Their Way with English Learners.* 1st ed. Upper Saddle River, NJ: Prentice Hall, 2006.

Bradlee, Charles. "The ABC Song." Boston, 1835.

Briggs, Anna. *ELPS Toolkit.* 2nd ed. Austin, TX: Region 13 Educational Service Center, 2015.

Classroom Clipart, http://classroomclipart.com/.

Clker, http://www.clker.com/.

The Electric Company, http://pbskids.org/electriccompany/.

Halliwell, James Orchard. "Here We Go Round the Mulberry Bush" England, 1850.

Montrose, Percy. "Oh My Darling, Clementine." USA, 1884.

Murphy, Raymond. *Essential Grammar in Use.* 4th ed. Cambridge, U.K.: Cambridge University Press, 2015.

PBS Learning Media, http://www.pbslearningmedia.org/.

Pitoniak, Mary J., John W. Young, Maria Mariniello, Teresa C. King, Alyssa Buteux, and Mitchell Ginsburgh. *Guidelines for the Assessment of English Language Learners.* Princeton, NJ: Educational Testing Service, 2009.

Public Domain Clip Art, http://www.pdclipart.org/.

Richards, Jack C., and Theodore S. Rogers. *Approaches and Methods in Language Teaching.* 3rd ed. Cambridge, U.K.: Cambridge University Press, 2014.

"Row, Row, Row, Your Boat." USA, 1852.

Teachers of English to Speakers of Other Languages, Inc. *PreK-12 English Language Proficiency Standards.* Alexandria, VA: TESOL, 2009.

"Three Blind Mice." England, 1805.

OTHER BOOKS BY STEPHANIE LERNER:

ESL for Beginners: Lessons Guide with Activities, Volume One

ESL for Beginners: Lessons Guide with Activities, Volume Two

ESL for Beginners: Lessons Guide with Activities, Volume Three

ESL in the Middle, Volume One: Lessons Guide for Teaching Intermediate English

ESL in the Middle, Volume Two: Lessons Guide for Teaching Intermediate English

ESL for Beginners – Culture Explorers

ESL Survival Skills – Exploring US Culture

¡Tranquila! Anger Management Counseling Guide with Spanish/English Activities

The Calm Downers: Anger Management Group Counseling Sessions Guide with Activities

Where There's a Goal, There's a Way: Individual Counseling Sessions Guide with Activities

¡GOL! Individual Counseling Sessions Guide with Spanish/English Activities

Cope Into Hope: Grief Counseling Guide with Activities

Bilingual Cope Into Hope: Grief Counseling Guide with Spanish/English Activities

The Broken Hearts Club: Grief Group Counseling Guide

Charla Entre Chicas: Bilingual Girl Empowerment Group Counseling Guide with Spanish/English Activities

Take It Easy: Stress Management Group Counseling Guide

Relajate: Bilingual Stress Management Group Counseling Guide with Spanish/English Activities

Get Your Goal On: Academic Success Group Counseling Guide

Goals Make the Man: Boys Leadership Group Counseling Guide

ESL Express: Lessons Guide for Teaching Beginning English

****

For information and free downloadable chapters on all Bilingual Learner books, go to www.bilinguallearner.com.

Like our Facebook page and to receive info about our other upcoming books.
www.instagram.com/bilinguallearner/
www.facebook.com/bilinguallearn/
www.pinterest.com/bilinguallearne/
www.twitter.com/bilinguallearn

About the Author Stephanie Lerner is a Johns Hopkins University-trained educator. She holds a BS in elementary education and an MS in counseling. With more than 20 years in both public and private education, she has Texas certifications in school counseling and bilingual/Spanish education. After traveling the world and teaching in such far off places as Mozambique and Bolivia, Stephanie came home to the United States to be a bilingual counselor and teacher in a high-need public school system. When she's not writing or educating, she enjoys ranch life with her husband and their menagerie of pets—all of whom are bilingual, of course!

Printed in Great Britain
by Amazon

36187396R10082